The Letters of St. Patrick and Early Patrician Literature

VOLUME VI

THE LIBRARY OF EARLY CHRISTIANITY

THE LIBRARY OF EARLY CHRISTIANITY

VOLUME VI

St. Patrick

The Letters of St. Patrick and Early Patrician Literature

Ancient text edited and translated by
PHILIP FREEMAN

The Catholic University of America Press
Washington, D.C.

The paper used in this publication meets the minimum
requirements of American National Standards for Information
Science—Permanence of Paper for Printed Library Materials,
ANSI Z39.48-1992.
∞

ISBN (paperback): 978-0-8132-3938-5
ISBN (eBook): 978-0-8132-3939-2

CONTENTS

Contents

ACKNOWLEDGMENTS

Philip Freeman

I am deeply grateful to the Catholic University of America Press for allowing me to present the letters of St. Patrick and the earliest works of the Patrician tradition to readers of the Library of Early Christianity series.

The libraries which preserve the seven medieval manuscripts of Patrick's letters were particularly kind in allowing me access to excellent photographic reproductions. My special thanks to Salisbury Cathedral for the superb digital photographs taken at my request. My thanks also to Joseph Nagy and Patrick Ford in the Celtic Languages and Literatures department at Harvard University, as well as Thomas O'Loughlin at the University of Wales, Lampeter.

I also greatly benefited from the resources of the libraries at Harvard University and Trinity College, Dublin. Many thanks as well to the National Endowment for the Humanities and the Loeb Classical Library Foundation for their financial support in my research.

Finally, I must express my profound gratitude to the late Ludwig Bieler whose exemplary work on Patrick and his commentators continues to provide the foundation of so much modern scholarship on early Latin literature in Ireland.

ABBREVIATIONS

BIBLICAL BOOKS

OT	Old Testament
Gn	Genesis
Ex	Exodus
Lv	Leviticus
Nm	Numbers
Dt	Deuteronomy
Jos	Joshua
Jgs	Judges
Ru	Ruth
1–2Sm	The first and second books of Samuel
1–2Kgs	The first and second books of Kings
1–2Chr	The first and second books of Chronicles
Ezr	Ezra
Neh	Nehemiah
Tb	Tobit
Est	Esther
Jdt	Judith
1–2Mc	The first and second books of Maccabees
Jb	Job
Ps(s)	Psalms
Prv	Proverbs
Eccl	Ecclesiastes
Song	Canticle of Canticles, Song of Songs
Wis	Wisdom of Solomon
Sir	Wisdom of Jesus ben Sirach, Ecclesiasticus

Abbreviations

Is	Isaiah
Jer	Jeremiah
Lam	Lamentations
Bar	Baruch
Ezek	Ezekiel
Dn	Daniel
Hos	Hosea
Jl	Joel
Am	Amos
Ob	Obadiah
Jon	Jonah
Mi	Micah
Na	Nahum
Hab	Habakkuk
Zep	Zephaniah
Hag	Haggai
Zec	Zechariah
Mal	Malachi
NT	New Testament
Mt	Matthew
Mk	Mark
Lk	Luke
Jn	John
Acts	Acts
Rom	The Epistle to the Romans
1–2Cor	The first and second Epistles to the Corinthians
Gal	The Epistle to the Galatians
Eph	The Epistle to the Ephesians
Phil	The Epistle to the Philippians
Col	The Epistle to the Colossians
1–2Thes	The first and second Epistles to the Thessalonians
1–2Tm	The first and second Epistles to Timothy

Abbreviations

Ti	The Epistle to Titus
Phlm	The Epistle to Philemon
Heb	The Epistle to the Hebrews
Jas	The Epistle of St. James
1–2Pt	The first and second Epistles of St. Peter
1–3Jn	The first through third Epistles of St. John
Jude	The Epistle of St. Jude
Rv	Apocalypse, Revelation

ANCIENT AND MEDIEVAL AUTHORS AND WORKS

ad ill.	Cyr., *Catecheses ad illuminandos 1–18*
A.I.	*The Annals of Inisfallen* (ed. Mac Airt, Dublin 1951)
Amm.	Ammianus Marcellinus
Antiph.	Antiphonary of Bangor
Ardm.	*Liber Ardmachanus (Book of Armagh)*
A. P.	Hor., *De Arte Poetica*
Ath.	Athanasius alexandrinus
A.U.	*The Annals of Ulster* (eds. Mac Airt and Mac Niocall, Dublin 1983)
Aug.	Augustinus episcopus hipponensis
Beda	Beda Venerabilis
Cassian.	Cassianus Abbas Massiliensis (Iohannes Cassianus)
Chron.	Prosp, *Epitoma Chronicorum*
Chrys.	Iohannes Chrysostomus
Cog.	Cogitosus
Coll.	Cassian., *Collationes*
Collec..	Tír., *Collectanea De. S. Patricio*
Conf.	Pk., *Confessio S. Patricii*
Cyr.	Cyrillus hierosolymitanus
De vir. inl.	Hier., *De viris inlustribus*
Don.	Aug., *Psalmus contra partem Donati*

Abbreviations

ep. episc.	Pk., *Epistula ad episcopos in Campo hAi* (fragm.)
ep. mil.	Pk., *Epistula ad milites Corotici*
Sym. epp.	Sym., *Epistulae*
Fast.	Ov., *Fastorum Libri Sex*
Heb. nom.	Hier, *Liber interpretationis hebraicorum nominum*
Hist ec.	*Historia ecclesiastica gentis Anglicorum*
Hier.	Hieronymus Presbyter (Jerome)
Hor.	Q. Horatius Flaccus
Hym. Sec.	Sec., *Hymn of Secundinus*
Hym. Pk.	Pk., *Hymnus S. Patricii*
In Hier.	Hier, *In Hieremiam prophetam 1. vi*
Lib. Hym.	Liber Hymnorum
Ov.	P. Ovidius Naso
Muir.	Muirchú
Myst.	Cyr., *Mystagogiae 1–5*
Pasc. Carm.	Sed., *Paschale Carmen*
Pk.	Patricius episcopus hibernorum
Prosp.	Prosper Aquitanus
Res Gest.	Amm., *Res Gestae*
Sec.	Secundinus
Sed.	Sedulius (Presbyter)
Sulp.	Sulpicius Severus
Sym.	Symmachus (Papa)
Syn.	Pk., *Synodus [i] episcoporum, id est Patricii, Auxilii et Isernini*
Tír.	Tírechán
VL	*Vetus Latina*
V. M.	Sulp., *Vita Martini Turonensis*
V. P.	Muir., *Vita S. Patricii*
V. A.	Ath., *Vita S. Antonii*
V. B.	Cogitosus, *Vita S. Brigidae*
Vulg.	*Vulgate*

Abbreviations

MODERN SERIES, PERIODICALS

ACO *Acta conciliorum oecumenicorum*

ACW Ancient Christian Writers

ADB *Allgemeine deutsche Biographie*

CSEL Corpus scriptorum ecclesiasticorum latinorum

IA *Irish Annals*

ICCS *International Congress of Celtic Studies*

MGH.AA Monumenta Germaniae historica, Auctores antiquissimi

PRIA *Proceedings of the Royal Irish Academy*

SC *Sources chrétiennes*

OTHER ABBREVIATIONS

ad loc. *ad locum* = on the aforementioned passage

ap. crit. *apparatus criticus* = the critical notes on the Greek text

ap. font. *apparatus fontium* = the apparatus of ancient sources

c. *circa* = approximately

cf. *confer* = compare

c. n. critical note (*i.e.* a note of the *ap. crit.*)

e.g. *exempli gratia* = for example

gr. *graecus*

i.e. *id est* = that is

lat. *latinus*

n. note

p(p). page(s)

rpt. reprint(ed)

sqq. *sequentes* = the following pp. or foll.

u. l. *uaria lectio* = variant reading

v. *uide* = see

INTRODUCTION TO PATRICK'S LIFE AND WORKS

1. THE LIFE OF PATRICK

What little reliable information we possess about Patrick's life comes from his two surviving letters. He was born Patricius, son of Calpornius, grandson of Potitus, in Roman Britain, probably in the closing years of the fourth century or the beginning of the fifth. His family owned a villa and was part of the local nobility, with his father serving as a Roman official at the otherwise unknown town of Bannaventa Berniae. His grandfather was a priest and his father a deacon, so we can be sure Patrick had a Christian upbringing, though he says he rejected the faith while still a child. As a teenager, he committed a serious but unnamed sin which caused him great trouble even as an old man when his church superiors discovered the deed. Sometime around his sixteenth birthday he was kidnapped by Irish slave raiders and taken back to Ireland where he endured six years of grueling slavery. During this time of servitude, he rediscovered his Christian faith and became a devout believer. In his early twenties, he reports that he heard the voice of God in a dream telling him to escape and flee back to Britain. Patrick followed the voice and risked his life to travel the length of Ireland to find a ship of pagan merchants who reluctantly accepted him as a passenger. Eventually he returned to his family in Britain, but there he experienced dreams calling him back to Ireland as a missionary. Patrick trained as a deacon, then priest, and finally returned to Ireland, eventually to become a bishop. His priestly training may have taken place in Gaul, perhaps at Auxerre, but it is more likely he studied with a bishop in Britain. His mission in Ireland lasted for many difficult years during which he suffered frequent persecution from Irish leaders and little

backing from church officials in Britain. At some point in his later years, some of his Irish converts were kidnapped and enslaved by a British warlord named Coroticus, prompting him to write his *Letter to the Soldiers of Coroticus*. Probably at a later date his relations with the British bishops reached a low point and he was recalled to answer charges of corruption, though Patrick vigorously denied these charges in his *Confession* and refused to leave Ireland, where he presumably died.

No contemporary documents mention Patrick or his mission. Prosper's *Chronicon* (Mommsen I.473) records that in 431, Pope Celestine sent the deacon Palladius "to the Irish believing in Christ." The Irish annals (A.I. 432, A.U. 432) record that Patrick arrived in the year 432 after the mission of Palladius failed, but this date is probably a later invention intended to have Patrick arrive on the island as soon as possible after Palladius. Patrick's date of death is recorded as March 17th, but the Irish annals variously give the year as 457, 461, 493, or 496 (A.I. 496, A.U. 457, 461, 493).

2. THE CIRCUMSTANCES AND COMPOSITION OF PATRICK'S LETTERS

The two surviving letters of Patrick were written under different circumstances when he was an old man in Ireland. His *Letter to the Soldiers of Coroticus* is a short, fiercely angry letter directed at the British tyrant and slave raider Coroticus who had kidnapped some and killed others of his Irish converts shortly after their baptism. Patrick accuses Coroticus and his men of murder and evil deeds against fellow Christians in the harshest terms, threatening God's wrath and quoting scripture throughout to support his case. In the letter Patrick urges British Christians to shun Coroticus and his followers unless they release their captives and make restitution immediately.

Patrick's longer letter, his *Confession*, is a spirited defense against charges brought against him by British church officials. The accusations included misuse of church funds and an unnamed sin committed by Patrick as a teenager which had recently come to light

through information provided by a longtime friend and confidant of Patrick's. We are fortunate that Patrick uses the occasion of the letter to tell the story of his early life and provide a glimpse of his unconventional missionary work in Ireland. As part of his defense, Patrick explains to the British church that spreading the gospel among the divided and warlike tribes of Ireland required unusual means that included payments to kings for safe passage through their territories. In the letter Patrick portrays Christian leaders in Britain as lacking sympathy for his work among the Irish. In the end, he refuses their summons to return to Britain and declares he will live out his remaining days among his Irish converts.

We cannot be certain which of Patrick's letters was written first, but there is a strong case to be made that the British bishops saw his *Letter to the Soldiers of Coroticus* as interfering in their ecclesiastical jurisdiction and thus prompted the accusations which led to his *Confession.*

In both letters, Patrick's frequent biblical quotations draw on the Old Latin Bible, but the manuscripts have often been regularized by later scribes to reflect the standard Vulgate edition of Jerome as was common practice (see White 1905, 230–33; Bieler 1993, 34–38).

3. THE MANUSCRIPTS OF PATRICK'S LETTERS

There are seven medieval manuscripts which preserve Patrick's letters wholly or in part. The earliest is *The Book of Armagh* (A) (fols. 22r–24v) now at Trinity College, Dublin, recorded by the scribe Ferdomnach at Armagh in 807. This manuscript contains only parts of the *Confession* and completely lacks the *Letter to the Soldiers of Coroticus.* Scholars vary in opinion on why certain sections of the *Confession* are missing in the *Book of Armagh,* though many believe it deliberately omits portions of the text in which Patrick admits his own failings. *The Book of Armagh* was later considered to have been transcribed by Patrick himself and was venerated as a sacred object at Armagh until the seventeenth century.

The other six manuscripts of Patrick's letters seem to have

originated with a single copy of both texts brought to northern France by an Irish monk during the seventh century. The well-preserved Paris manuscript (P) (fols. 72r–85v), dating perhaps to the tenth century, contains the earliest complete copy of both letters. It was transferred to Paris from the abbey of Saint-Corneille in nearby Compiègne during Napoleon's reign.

The twelfth-century manuscript from Arras (V) (fols. 50v–53r) contained the full text of both letters until two leaves were lost in early modern times. The municipal library at Rouen possesses a badly damaged and incomplete text (R) (157v–159v) of the *Confession* only from the eleventh century which may have originated at the Benedictine abbey at Jumièges. The three surviving British manuscripts also owe their origins to northern France. The British Museum houses a complete text (C) (169v–174v) from Worchester dating to the early eleventh century, while Salisbury cathedral preserves two manuscripts (F) (7r–13r) and (G) (158r–166r) lately of Oxford which date to the twelfth century.

The variants in the manuscripts generally fall between A and the other six as a group (F). Within this group, P stands apart, as does V, from RFCG (D). A and P usually provide the best readings. The number of recensions between the archetype (S) and the branches A and F is difficult to determine. For a detailed discussion of the manuscripts, see Bieler (1993, 7–34). A simplified stemma would be as follows:

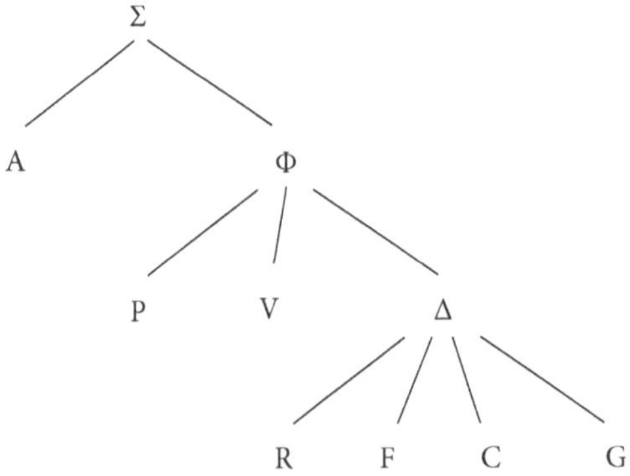

4. PREVIOUS EDITIONS OF PATRICK'S LETTERS AND MODERN SCHOLARSHIP

Patrick's letters were first edited by Sir James Ware in his *S. Patricio adscripta opera* (London 1656) and by Daniel Papebroch in the *Acta sanctorum* (Anvers 1668). Both these editions, though remarkable for their time, suffer from a limited use of the surviving medieval manuscripts. The few editions of the next two centuries were similar in their restricted use of available manuscripts. Newport White's *Libri Sancti Patricii* (Dublin 1905) brought the letters of Patrick into modern scholarship with his careful review of all the available manuscripts and his impressive philological skill. His subsequent 1918 revision incorporated the Paris manuscript as well as minor changes in format. Sixty years ago, Ludwig Bieler produced the *Libri Epistolarum Sancti Patricii* (Dublin 1952, revised 1993), still the standard edition of Patrick's letters and a remarkable work which has endured in the controversial realm of Patrician scholarship for over half a century. With only minor modifications which I note, I have taken Bieler's text as the standard for this edition of Patrick's letters. Richard Hanson and Cécile Blanc have also produced an admirable Latin-French edition of Patrick's letters, *Confession et Lettre à Coroticus* (Paris 1978).

There have been numerous studies of Patrick and his letters over the last century. A few of the most important works include John Bury's *Life of St. Patrick and his Place in History* (London 1905), James Carney's *The Problem of St. Patrick* (Dublin 1973), R.P.C. Hanson's *Saint Patrick: His Origins and Career* (Oxford 1968), E.A. Thompson's *Who Was Saint Patrick?* (Woodbridge 1985), David Dumville's *Saint Patrick A.D. 493–1993* (Woodbridge 1993), Thomas O'Loughlin's *Discovering Saint Patrick* (New York 2005), and Roy Flechner's *Saint Patrick Retold* (Princeton, 2012). The latter three works contain a substantial bibliography of recent Patrician scholarship.

INTRODUCTION TO EARLY PATRICIAN LITERATURE

1. MUIRCHÚ'S *LIFE OF ST. PATRICK*

Muirchú maccu Machtheni was an Irish churchman from the region of Armagh who recorded the first and most influential life story of Patrick in the late seventh century. We know little about him, aside from the few facts he reveals in his writing, except that he was present at the Synod of Birr in 697.

Muirchú dedicated his *Life of Patrick* to Bishop Áed of Sléibte (Sleaty) in northern Leinster, perhaps in an effort to win that diocese to the growing ecclesiastical power of Armagh. Muirchú was writing at a time when the cult of Patrick was expanding, along with the power of the church at Armagh and the political reach of the Uí Néill dynasty in the northern part of Ireland. All three of these movements were tied closely together and supported one another. It is therefore tempting to see Muirchú's writing as little more than propaganda, but this would be too cynical a view. His *Life* certainly is a work of ecclesiastical maneuvering on the part of the church at Armagh, but it also came at a time in Irish history when Christians were beginning to look back at their own history. Two hundred years had passed since the death of Patrick and most of the country had become firmly Christian. There was a curiosity and hunger for stories about the beginnings of their faith among clergy and laity alike.

Muirchú's *Life* is well within the hagiographical tradition found on the continent. The *Life of St. Martin* by Sulpicius Severus and Athanasius' account of St. Anthony were well-known in Ireland by the seventh century. The *Life of St. Brigid of Kildare* composed by the churchman Cogitosus had already appeared in Ireland before

Muirchú. Like all hagiography, the intent of the author was not to record an accurate biography of his subject but to inspire readers to lives of holiness. Muirchú knew of Patrick's letters or at least a source closely based on them, but he feels perfectly free to change the facts when it suits his purpose. The simple voice of the unknown Victoricus calling to Patrick in a dream (*Confession* 23) becomes the continuing presence of the angel Victor in Muirchú's version (1.1), while the British tyrant Coroticus of Patrick's *Letter* in Muirchú's text is changed into a fox after Patrick prays for God's vengeance to fall upon him (1.29). Indeed, Muirchú's work is full of miracle stories and solemn contests of good versus evil inspired by Moses before Pharaoh and Elijah defeating the prophets of Baal (Exodus 5–15; 1 Kings 18). In Muirchú, Patrick becomes the ideal missionary bishop converting pagans to Christ with signs and wonders. The very human Patrick of the letters is lost beneath the miracles stories of Muirchú, but again it would be a profound mistake to see Muirchú as a failed biographer. The great popularity of the *Life* in the Middle Ages in Ireland and beyond is proof enough that Muirchú succeeded in his goals for the work.

Muirchú's *Life* is preserved in three manuscripts, none of which is complete. The *Book of Armagh* (fols. 2r–8r) contains the best text, though it is missing the introductory material. An eleventh-century manuscript now in Brussels (Bibliothèque royale 64, fols. 299r–303r) lacks the later material but preserves the opening chapters. Two eighth-century fragments from Austria (Vienna, Nationalbibliothek Ser. nov. 3642) contain only a small portion of the text. As far as can be determined, Muirchú used the Vulgate rather than the Old Latin Bible.

The original order of chapters in Muirchú's *Life* is debated by scholars and an analysis of the problem is beyond the limited scope of this edition. I have followed Ludwig Bieler's 1979 edition, in which he provides extensive commentary on the text and tradition. Other recent works on Muirchú include Hood (1978, 1–22, 61–98), Dumville (1993, 203–19), (De Paor 175–97), and O'Loughlin (2005, 112–30, 192–229).

2. TÍRECHÁN'S *JOURNEY OF ST. PATRICK*

Tírechán was a bishop and native of Tír-Amolngid, modern Tirawley in northwest County Mayo. We know very little about his life except that he was a disciple of Bishop Ultán moccu Conchobuir at Ardbraccan near Navan in County Mayo. According to the annals, Ultán died in 657, just before a great plague struck Ireland in 664. Tírechán mentions this plague in his narrative, so that the date of his work is sometime after this event, probably in the 670's.

Unlike Muirchú, Tírechán is not so much interested in miracle stories of Patrick as he is in establishing that various churches throughout Ireland were founded by and therefore owe their allegiance to the saint. He states that some of his information comes from a book of Ultán and from discussions with his mentor, but much of the material was gathered locally by Tírechán on travels he himself made to the places he mentions in his text. The roundabout journey of Patrick Tírechán records from Meath to Connaught, Ulster, and Leinster is scarcely logical and is certainly pure invention on Tírechán's part to provide a framework for his story. Although Patrick may have visited some of the places Tírechán mentions, we have no reliable information for the missionary travels of the saint. Whether or not Tírechán knew Muirchú or if his work was written before his contemporary's *Life* is unknown. The two generally agree on actions of Patrick that both mention, though it is likely they are drawing on a common source or sources.

Tírechán's *Journey* (the author gives no title) is found only in the *Book of Armagh* (9r–16r), in the folios following Muirchú's *Life*. There are notable gaps in sections of the narrative and the text is corrupt in others. I have again followed the 1979 edition of Bieler and noted those few points where I differ from him. The abundance of personal and place names mentioned in the text prohibit a full discussion and identification, though many are unknown or uncertain in any case. Only the major figures, places, and terms have been mentioned in the notes. A full discussion can be found in Bieler's textual commentary. Modern translations include the corresponding section of

Bieler's text, as well as De Paor (1993, 154–74), which is particularly good with place names. Kenney (1929, 329–31) has a brief but excellent discussion of Tírechán's background and methods.

3. *THE SAYINGS OF ST. PATRICK*

The *Dicta Patricii* are three short sayings inserted in the *Book of Armagh* (fol. 9r) by the scribe Ferdomnach and found only in that manuscript. The only one of certain veracity is the second, taken directly from Patrick's *Letter* (17). They occur just before the text of Tírechán's *Journey of St. Patrick* (see Bieler 1979, 124–25) and were likely found in the exemplar of Tírechán used by Ferdomnach. Opinion has varied on whether or not to accept the first and third sayings as genuine (see Kenney 1929, 334; Bieler 1953A, 95–96; De Paor 1993, 202; O'Loughlin 2005, 184–85).

4. *THE FIRST SYNOD OF ST. PATRICK*

This brief document of thirty-four canons or rules is a circular letter attributed to Patrick and his traditional auxiliary bishops Auxilius and Iserninus, but it likely dates to a century or two after Patrick. An early date of composition is probable due to the references (8, 13, 14, 20) to a still-flourishing pagan society in Ireland, as well as the non-Vulgate quotation in its prologue. It is the earliest surviving document from Ireland dealing with ecclesiastical discipline.

The text is found in a single manuscript, Corpus Christi College, Cambridge 279, written in one hand and dating to the ninth or tenth century. The subject matter of the letter is primarily the proper role of clergy and the jurisdiction of bishops, though several canons deal with lay members of the Christian community, especially in their relations with non-Christians.

The standard modern edition is found in Bieler's *The Irish Penitentials* (1975, 54–59). *The Bishop's Synod*, a symposium publication with Latin text, translation, and extensive notes edited by M. J. Faris (1976) is also most helpful.

5. *THE HYMN OF ST. SECUNDINUS*

From about 800, this hymn has been attributed to Secundinus, Sechnall in Irish, who was considered a contemporary and helper of St. Patrick in his missionary work. The Irish annals record that he joined Patrick in Ireland in 439 and died in 447/448 (A.I. 439, 447, A.U. 439, 447). Neither his dates nor the tradition of his authorship can be considered reliable, but the hymn's early date is established by its earliest manuscript occurrence in the *Antiphonary of Bangor* in the late seventh century.

In Latin, the first stanza of this hymn begins *Audite omnes* ("Hear everyone") and continues as an abecedarian hymn with following stanzas each beginning with a consecutive letter of the alphabet, in the tradition of Psalm 118 or Augustine's *Psalmus contra partem Donatii*. Each of the twenty-three stanzas is four lines long with fifteen syllables per line. In spite of its somewhat repetitive nature, the hymn was evidently popular in early Ireland and may be the hymn recommended by Muirchú (2.6) to believers on the day of their death that they might be judged by Patrick himself.

The hymn is preserved in five medieval manuscripts. Aside from the *Antiphonary of Bangor* (Milan, Ambros. C5 fol. 13v-15v), it is found in two eleventh-century copies of the Irish book of hymns known as the *Liber Hymnorum*: Trinity College, 1441 (fol. 1r–2v) and Franciscan Library, Killiney, A.2 (p. 12–15). It also found in the *Leabhar Breac* at the Royal Irish Academy (23.P.16, p. 238b), written before 1411. The last three stanza are also preserved in an 11th-century manuscript at Corpus Christi College in Cambridge (41, p. 207). I have used Bieler's text of 1953, the standard modern edition, which relies primarily on the manuscript in the *Antiphonary of Bangor*. See also Kenney (1929, 258–60) and O'Loughlin (2005, 186–91).

6. *ST. PATRICK'S BREASTPLATE*

This brief morning prayer in Old Irish invoking divine protection and attributed to Patrick is found in the *Liber Hymnorum* (Trinity College, 42, fol. 19v). The date of its original composition is uncertain, but probably the sixth or seventh centuries. It was clearly written at a time when the influence of the pagan druids was still very much alive in Ireland.

The story in the preface of prayer relates that it was used by Patrick to ward of evil when he faced King Loegaire at Tara. It reputedly turned him and his companions into deer, hence the Irish name for the prayer, the *Fáeth Fiada* or "Deer's Cry," though it is known by the Latin term *Lorica* or "Breastplate." There are a number of such breastplate prayers or *loricae* in both Irish and Latin from the early period. The theme of invocations against evil certainly goes back to pre-Christian Celtic times, but the concept is also found in the New Testament (e.g. Eph 6.11, 1Thes 5.8). The standard edition of the prayer is found in *Thesaurus Palaeohibernicus* vol. 2, xxxv, xl, 354–58. See also Kenney 1929, 272–74; Bieler 1953A, 67–72.

BIBLIOGRAPHY

Bible: Ancient Texts, Versions, Concordance

Ancient Texts and Versions

Old Latin Bible (Vetus Latina)

Sebatier, P., *Vetus Italica*, 1743–49.

Archabbey of Beuron, *Vetus Latina*, 1949–present.

Vulgate

Weber, R., and R. Gryson, *Biblia sacra iuxta vulgatam versionem*, 4th ed. (Stuttgart 1994)

ANCIENT AUTHORS AND WORKS: TEXTS, TRANSLATIONS, COMMENTARIES

A. Patricii opera

Bieler, L., *Libri Epistolarum Sancti Patricii Episcopi: Introduction, Text, and Commentary* (Dublin 1952; rpt. 1993)

Freeman, P. *The World of Saint Patrick* (Oxford 2014)

Hanson, R. and C. Blanc, *Confession et lettre à Coroticus* (Paris 1978)

Hood, A.B.E., *St. Patrick: His Writings and Muirchú's Life* (London 1978)

Papebroch, D. *De Sancto Patricio Episcopo Apostolo et Primate Hiberniae* (Anvers 1668)

Ware, J., *S. Patricio qui Hibernos ad fidem Christi converity, adscripta opuscula* (London 1656)

White, N.J.D., "Libri Sancti Patricii: The Latin Writings of Saint Patrick" in *Proceedings of the Royal Irish Academy* (Dublin 1905) = *PRIA* vol. 25 (Section C) (1905), pp. 201–326.

_______, *A Translation of the Latin Writings of St. Patrick*, in *Texts for Students* vol. 5 (London, 1918)

B. De Patricio opera

Bieler, L., "The Hymn of St. Secundinus" in *Proceedings of the Royal Irish Academy* (Dublin 1953) = *PRIA* vol. 55 (1953), pp. 117–27

_______, *The Works of St. Patrick, St. Secundinus: Hymn on St. Patrick* (New York 1953)

_______, *The Irish Penitentials* (Dublin 1963)

_______, *The Patrician Texts in the Book of Armagh* (Dublin 1979)

Faris, M.J., *The Bishop's Synod* (Liverpool 1976)

Stokes, W., and Strachan, J., eds. "Patrick's Hymn" in *Thesaurus Paleohibernicus* 2, 354–58 (Cambridge 1903).

C. Other Ancient Authors and Works

Ammianus Marcellinus

Res Gestae

Seyfarth, W., *Rerum Gestarum Libri Qui Supersunt* (Leipzig 1973)

Athanasius alexandrinus

Vita S. Antonii

Bartelink, G. J. M., *Athanase D'Alexandrie: Vie D'Antoine* SC 400 (Paris 1994)

Beda

Historia ecclesiastica gentis Anglicorum

Colgrave, B. and R.A.B. Mynors, *Bede's Ecclesiastical History Of The English People* (Clarendon 1969)

Cassianus Abbas Massiliensis (Iohannes Cassianus)

Collationes

Petschenig, M., *Iohannis Casssiani Opera*, part 2: *Conlationes XXIIII*, CSEL, vol. 13 (Vienna 1886)

Cogitosus

Vita S. Brigidae

Socii Bollandiani edd., *Acta Sanctorum, Vita S. Brigidae auctore Cogitoso*, Febr. i. (1863) pp. 135–41

Bibliography

Cyrillus hierosolymitanus

Mystagogiae

Piedagnel, A. and P. Paris, *Cyrille de Jérusalem. Catéchèses mystagogiques* (Paris 1988)

Hieronymus Presbyter

De viris inlustribus

Richardson, E. C., "Hieronymus: Liber De Viris Inlustribus" in *Texte und Untersuchungen zur Geschichte der Altchristlichen Literatur* vol. 14 (Leipzig 1896)

In Hieremiam prophetam

Reiter, S., *S. Evsebii Hieronymi Opera*, sect. 2 part 1: *In Hieremiam Prophetam Libri Sex*, CSEL, vol. LIX (Vienna 1913; rpt. Wiesbaden, Germany 1961)

Liber interpretationis hebraicorum nominum

de Lagarde, P., *Hebraicae quaestiones in libro Geneseos. Liber interpretationis hebraicorum nominum* etc., CChr.SL, vol. LXXII (Turnhout 1999)

(Q.) Horatius Flaccus

De Arte Poetica

Borzsák, S., *Q. Horati Flacci Opera* (Leipzig 1984) pp. 292–312

(P.) Ovidius Naso

Fastorum Libri Sex

Alton, E.H., et al., *P. Ovidi Nasonis Fastorum Libri Sex* (Leipzig 1978)

Prosper Aquitanus

Epitoma Chronicorum

Mommsen, T., "Prosperi Tironis Epitoma Chronicon," in MGH.AA, tom 9: Chronica minora, saec. IV-VII, vol. 1 (Berlin 1892), pp. 341–499

Sedulius (Presbyter)

Paschale Carmen

Huemer, J. *Sedulii Opera* CSEL, vol. 10 (Vienna 1885) pp. 1–154

Bibliography

Sulpicius Severus

Vita Martini Turonensis

Fontaine, J., *Sulpice Sévère: Vie de Saint Martin*, 2 voll., SC 133 (Paris 1967)

Symmachus (Quintus Aurelius)

Epistulae

Seeck, O., *Q. Aurelii Symmachi quae Supersunt*, MGH.AA, vol. 6.1 (Berlin 1883)

Other Works

Antiphonary of Bangor

Warren, F. E., *The Antiphonary of Bangor, An Early Irish Manuscript in the Ambrosian Library at Milan* (London 1895)

Liber Hymnorum

Bernard, J. H. and R. Atkinson, *The Irish Liber Hymnorum* (London 1898)

B. Secondary Works: Dictionaries, Monographs, Essays, Articles

Bowersock, G.W., Peter Brown, and Oleg Grabar. *Late Antiquity: A Guide to the Postclassical World* (Cambridge, MA 1999)

Bury, J., *Life of St. Patrick and his Place in History* (London 1905)

Carney, J., *The Problem of St. Patrick* (Dublin 1973)

Collingwood, R.G. and R.P. Wright, *The Roman Inscriptions of Britain* (Oxford 1965)

Concannon, H., "Silva Focluti, Silva Uluti, or Silva Virgulti?" in *Féil-Sgríbhinn Éoin Mhic Néill: Essays and Studies Presented to Proferssor Eoin MacNeill* (Dublin 1940)

De Paor, L., *Saint Patrick's World* (Notre Dame 1993)

Dumville, D., *Saint Patrick, A.D. 493–1993* (Woodbridge 1993)

Flechner, R. *Saint Patrick Retold: The Legend and History of Ireland's Patron Saint* (Princeton 2021)

Freeman, P. *Saint Patrick of Ireland* (New York, 2005)

Hanson, R.P.C., *Saint Patrick: His Origins and Career* (Oxford 1968)

Bibliography

Hood, A.B.E., *St. Patrick: His Writings and Muirchu's Life* (London 1978)

James, E., *The Franks* (Oxford 1988)

Kelly, F., *A Guide to Early Irish Law* (Dublin 1988)

Kenney, J. *The sources for the early history of Ireland* (New York 1929)

Maier, B., "Sugere mammellas: A Pagan Irish Custom and its Affiliates" in *Celtic connections: proceedings of the Tenth International Congress of Celtic Studies* (East Linton 1999) = *ICCS* vol. 10 (1999), pp. 152–61

O'Loughlin, T., *Discovering Saint Patrick* (London 2005)

Rivet, A.L.F and C. Smith, *The Place-Names of Roman Britain* (Princeton 1979)

Stokes, W. and John Strachan, *Thesaurus Palaeohibernicus: a collection of Old-Irish glosses, Scholia prose, and verse.* (Cambridge 1901)

Thompson, E.A., *Who Was Saint Patrick?* (New York 1985)

CONSPECTUS SIGLORUM

1. THE MANUSCRIPTS OF ST. PATRICK'S LETTERS

A *Book of Armagh*, Trinity College, Dublin 52

Written *c.* 807 in part by the scribe Ferdomnach of Armagh. Contains only the *Confession* with gaps (22r–24v)

P Paris, Bibliothèque Nationale, Latin 17626

10th century, transferred to the Bibliothèque Nationale from Saint-Corneille, Compiègne in 1802. Contains full text of *Confession* and *Epistle* (72r–85v)

V Arras, Bibliothèque Municipale 450

12th century, written in northern France, perhaps at Saint-Vaast, Arras. Two missing leaves, but contains both letters (50v–53r)

C British Museum, Cotton Nero E1

c. 1000, probably written at Worchester. Preserves full text of both letters (169v–174v)

R Rouen, Bibliothèque Municipale 1391

11th century, badly damaged copy of *Confession* only (157v–159v)

G Salisbury Cathedral Library 221 (formerly Oxford, Bodleian Library, Fell 4)

12th century, written at Salisbury, contains entire text of both letters (158r–166r)

F Salisbury Cathedral Library 223 (formerly Oxford, Bodleian Library, Fell 3)

12th century, written at Salisbury, contains entire text of both letters (7r–13r)

2. MANUSCRIPTS OF PATRICIAN LITERATURE

Muirchú's *Life of St. Patrick*

A *Book of Armagh*, Trinity College, Dublin 52, *c.* 807 (2r–8v).

B Brussels, Bibliothèque Royale 64, 11th century (299r–303r).

C Vienna, Nationalbibliothek Ser. nov. 3642.

Conspectus siglorum

Tírechán's *Journey of St. Patrick*

A *Book of Armagh*, Trinity College, Dublin 52, *c.* 807 (9r–15v)

The Sayings of St. Patrick

A *Book of Armagh*, Trinity College, Dublin 52, *c.* 807 (9r)

The First Synod of St. Patrick

C Corpus Christi College, Cambridge 279, 9/10th century (1r–5v)

Hymn of St. Secundinus

A *Antiphonary of Bangor*, Milan, Ambros. C.5, 680–691 (13v–15v)

T *Liber Hymnorum*, Trinity College, Dublin 1441 (E.4.2), 11th century (1r–2v)

F *Liber Hymnorum*, Killiney, Franciscan House of Studies A.2, 11/12th century (12–15)

B *Leabhar Breac*, Dublin, Royal Irish Academy, 23.P.16, before 1411 (238b)

St. Patrick's Breastplate

T *Liber Hymnorum*, Trinity College, Dublin 1441 (E.42), 11th century

F *Liber Hymnorum*, Killiney, Franciscan House of Studies A.2, 11/12th century

3. PRIOR EDITIONS

Works of St. Patrick

War. J. Ware, *S. Patricio ascripta opera*

Pap. D. Papebroch, *Acta sanctorum*

Whi. N. White, *Libri Sancti Patricii*

Whi.[2] N. White, 1918 Revision of *Libri Sancti Patricii*

Bie. L. Bieler, *Libri Epistolorum Sancti Patricii*

Han. R. Hanson and C. Blanc, *Confession et Lettre à Coroticus*

Works about St. Patrick

Hoo. A. B. E. Hood, *St. Patrick: His Writings and Muirchu's Life*

Bie.^{2} L. Bieler, *The Irish Penitentials*

Bie.^{3} L. Bieler, *The Patrician Texts in the Book of Armagh*

Far. *The Bishop's Synod*

4. EDITORIAL ABBREVIATIONS

ac *ante correctionem*

coni. *coniecit* (*i.e.*, suggested an emendation but did not introduce it into the text)[1]

edd. *editores*

homotel. *homoteleuton*

om. *omisit*

pc *post correctionem* (*i.e.*, by either the first or another hand)

scr. *scripsit, -erunt* (*i.e.*, inserted an emendation into the text)[2]

signif. *significauit*

suppl. *suppleuit*

X^{-3} the concurrent reading of all mss. of class *X* with the exception of X^3

? perhaps

/ illegible letter

[ ] interpolation in the text

< > encloses a word or phrase added by the editor

+ + encloses a textual corruption with no likely conjectural remedy

*** marks an undoubted gap in the text

[***] marks a conjectured gap in the text

1. In cases where more than one editor is named after *coni.*, the first is to be credited with the suggestion, with which the following has/have concurred.

2. In cases where more than one editor is named after *scr.*, the first is to be credited with introducing the emendation into the text; the following has/have concurred.

The Letters of St. Patrick and Early Patrician Literature

EPISTULA AD MILITES COROTICI

(1) Patricius peccator indoctus scilicet Hiberione constitutus episcopum me esse fateor. Certissime reor a Deo accepi id quod sum. Inter barbaras itaque gentes habito proselitus et profuga ob amorem Dei; testis est ille si ita est. Non quod optabam tam dure et tam aspere aliquid ex ore meo effundere; sed cogor zelo Dei, et ueritas Christi excitauit, pro dilectione proximorum atque filiorum, pro quibus tradidi patriam et parentes et *animam meam usque ad mortem.*[a] Si dignus sum, uiuo Deo meo docere gentes etsi contempnor aliquibus.

(2) Manu mea scripsi atque condidi uerba ista danda et tradenda, militibus mittenda Corotici, non dico ciuibus meis neque ciuibus sanctorum Romanorum sed ciuibus daemoniorum, ob mala opera ipsorum. Ritu hostili in morte uiuunt, socii Scottorum atque Pictorum apostatorum. Sanguilentos sanguinare de sanguine innocentium Christianorum, quos ego in numero Deo genui atque in Christo confirmaui!

(3) Postera die qua crismati neophyti in ueste candida—flagrabat in fronte ipsorum dum crudeliter trucidati atque mactati gladio supradictis—misi epistolam cum sancto presbytero quem ego ex infantia docui, cum clericis, ut nobis aliquid indulgerent de praeda uel de captiuis baptizatis quos ceperunt: cachinnos fecerunt de illis.

a. Cf. Phil 2.30.

ST. PATRICK'S *LETTER TO THE SOLDIERS OF COROTICUS*

(1) I, Patrick, a sinner and very ignorant man, declare that I am established as a bishop in Ireland. Certainly I believe that what I am I have received from God. I live among barbarians and pagans as a stranger and exile for the love of God. He is my witness that this is the truth. I have never wished to speak harshly and sternly, but the zeal of God and the truth of Christ have forced me to do so—for the sake of my neighbors and sons for whom I gave up my homeland, my family, and "my very life until death." If I am worthy, I live for my God to teach unbelievers, even if some despise me.

(2) With my own hand I have written and composed these words, to be given, handed over, and sent to the soldiers of Coroticus. I do not say to my countrymen or to the blessed Roman citizens, but to those who by their evil deeds have become fellow citizens of the demons. Behaving like our enemies they live in death, allies of the Irish[1] and the apostate Picts.[2] They are bloodthirsty men yearning for the blood of innocent Christians—those I brought to life in God and confirmed in Christ!

(3) On the day after these men cruelly cut down my newly baptized—still wearing their white robes, still with the anointing oil on their foreheads[3]—I sent them a letter carried by a holy priest whom I had trained since his youth, along with some clerics, asking that they return the baptized captives along with some of the stolen loot—but they only laughed.

1. *Scotti* is the name for the Irish used from the fourth century AD. (cf. Ammianus Marcellinus 20.1).

2. The Picts, who lived in northern Britain beyond Roman control, were evangelized by Ninian beginning in the early fifth century (Bede 3.4). Some of them, called apostates by Patrick, had apparently drifted from Christian teachings.

3. The anointing of newly baptized Christians with oil blessed by a bishop or priest and the wearing of a white tunic representing purity became standard practice in the east and west by the fourth century (Cyril of Jerusalem, *Catechetical Lectures*. 21.3, 22.8).

(4) Idcirco nescio quid magis lugeam: an qui interfecti uel quos ceperunt uel quos grauiter zabulus inlaqueauit. Perenni poena gehennam pariter cum ipso mancipabunt, quia utique *qui facit peccatum seruus est*[b] et *filius zabuli*[c] nuncupatur.

(5) Quapropter resciat omnis homo timens Deum quod a me alieni sunt et a Christo Deo meo, *pro quo legationem fungor*,[d] patricida, fratricida, *lupi rapaces*[e] *deuorantes plebem* Domini *ut cibum panis,*[f] sicut ait: *Iniqui dissipauerunt legem tuam*[g], *Domine*, quam in supremis temporibus Hiberione optime benigne plantauerat atque instructa erat fauente Deo.

(6) Non usurpo. Partem habeo cum his *quos aduocauit et praedestinauit*[h] euangelium praedicare in persecutionibus non paruis *usque ad extremum terrae*[i], etsi inuidet inimicus per tyrannidem Corotici, qui Deum non ueretur nec sacerdotes ipsius, quos elegit et indulsit illis summam diuinam sublimam potestatem, *quos ligarent super terram ligatos esse et in caelis.*[j]

(7) Vnde ergo quaeso plurimum, *sancti et humiles corde,*[k] adulari talibus non licet *nec cibum* nec potum *sumere*[l] cum ipsis nec elemosinas ipsorum recipi debeat donec crudeliter paenitentiam effusis lacrimis satis Deo faciant et liberent seruos Dei et ancillas Christi baptizatas, pro quibus mortuus est et crucifixus.

(8) *Dona iniquorum reprobat Altissimus. Qui offert sacrificium ex substantia pauperum quasi qui uictimat filium in conspectu patris sui.*[m] *Diuitias*, inquit, *quas congregauit iniuste euomentur de uentre eius, trahit illum angelus mortis, ira draconum mulcabitur, interficiet illum lingua colubris, comedit autem eum ignis inextinguibilis.*[n] Ideoque: *Vae qui replent se quae non sunt sua,*[o] uel: *Quid*

b. Jn 8:34 c. Cf. Jn 8:44. d. Eph 6.20 e. Mt 7.15 ; cf. Acts 20.29.
f. Ps 13.4, 52.5 g. Ps 118.126 h. Rom 8.30 i. Acts 13.47
j. Mt. 16.19 k. Dn 3.87 l. Cf. 1 Cor 5.11. m. Sir 34.23–24
n. Jb 20.15–16, 26 o. Hab 2.6

(4) I do not know for whom I should weep more: those who were killed, those who were captured, or those so thoroughly trapped in the snares of Satan. Together with him they will suffer eternal punishment in Hell, for "whoever commits sin is its slave" and will be called "a son of Satan."

(5) Because of this, let everyone who fears God know that these men are strangers to me and to Christ my God, "whom I serve as an ambassador." Murderers of fathers and brothers! "Ravaging wolves who devour the people of God like bread!" As the Scripture says: The wicked "have destroyed your law, O Lord." The law which God in his mercy and kindness has established in Ireland in these last days.

(6) I am not exceeding my authority. I am one of those "whom he called and predestined" to preach the gospel in spite of fearsome persecutions "to the very ends of the earth," even if the enemy shows his jealousy through the tyrant Coroticus, a man who has no respect for God or his priests. God has chosen these priests and given to them the highest, divine, and sublime power, that "whomever they bind on earth will also be bound in heaven."

(7) Therefore I earnestly plead with all of you who are "holy and humble of heart." It is not right to seek the favor of such men nor "to eat bread" or drink with them. Don't even take charity from them until they in tearful remorse repent before God and free the servants of God and the baptized handmaids of Christ, those for whom He was crucified and died.

(8) "The Lord rejects the gifts of the wicked. Whoever offers sacrifice from the goods of the poor is like someone who sacrifices a son in the sight of his father." "Riches," He says, "which someone gathers unjustly, will be vomited out of his belly. The angel of death will seize him, angry dragons will crush him, the bite of the viper will kill him, and unquenchable fire will devour him." Therefore: "Woe to those who fill themselves with what is not theirs," and:

prodest homini ut totum mundum lucretur et animae suae detrimentum patiatur?[p]

(9) Longum est per singula discutere uel insinuare, per totam legem carpere testimonia de tali cupiditate: Auaritia mortale crimen. *Non concupisces rem proximi tui.*[q] *Non occides.*[r] Homicida non potest esse cum Christo. *Qui odit fratrem suum homicida*[s] adscribitur. Vel: *Qui non diligit fratrem suum in morte manet.*[t] Quanto magis reus est qui manus suas coinquinauit in sanguine filiorum Dei, quos nuper adquisiuit in ultimis terrae per exhortationem paruitatis nostrae?

(10) Numquid sine Deo uel secundum carnem Hiberione ueni? Quis me compulit? *Alligatus* sum *Spiritu*[u] ut non uideam aliquem de cognatione mea. Numquid a me piam misericordiam quod ago erga gentem illam qui me aliquando ceperunt et deuastauerunt seruos et ancillas domus patris mei? Ingenuus fui secundum carnem; decorione patre nascor. Vendidi enim nobilitatem meam—non erubesco neque me paenitet—pro utilitate aliorum; denique seruus sum in Christo genti exterae ob gloriam ineffabilem *perennis uitae quae est in Christo Iesu Domino nostro.*[v]

(11) Et si mei me non cognoscunt, *propheta in patria sua honorem non habet.*[w] Forte non sumus *ex* uno *ouili*[x] neque *unum Deum patrem habemus,*[y] sicut ait: *Qui non est mecum contra me est, et qui non congregat mecum spargit.*[z] Non conuenit: *Vnus destruit, alter aedificat.*[aa] *Non quaero quae mea sunt.*[ab] Non mea gratia sed Deus *qui dedit hanc sollicitudinem in corde meo*[ac] ut unus essem *de uenatoribus siue piscatoribus*[ad] quos olim Deus *in nouissimis diebus*[ae] ante praenuntiauit.

p. Mt 16.26 q. Ex 20.17 r. Ex 20.13 s. 1Jn 3.15
t. 1Jn 3.14 u. Acts 20.22 v. Rom 6.23 w. Jn 4.44
x. Cf. Jn 10.16. y. Jn 8.41 z. Mt 12.30 aa. Sir 34.28
ab. Cf. 1Cor 13.5. ac. 2Cor 8.16 ad. V. Jer 16.16. ae. Acts 2.17, etc.

"What profit is there for a man to gain the whole world but suffer the loss of his own soul?"

(9) It would take too long to list and set forth all the passages of the law condemning such greed: Avarice is a deadly sin. "You shall not desire the goods of your neighbor." "Do not murder." A murderer cannot be with Christ. "Whoever hates his brother" is counted as "a murderer." Or: "Whoever does not love his brother remains in death." How much worse is a man who stains his own hands with the blood of God's children, those He has recently acquired at the ends of the earth through me—insignificant as I am?

(10) Did I come to Ireland without the help of God or according to the flesh? Who forced me? I am "bound by the Spirit" so that I cannot see my own family. Is it of my own doing that I feel this holy mercy towards a people who once enslaved me and killed so many servants, both men and women, from my father's household? I am a freeborn man by the reckoning of this world; I am the son of a decurion.[4] But I sold my nobility—I am not ashamed nor do I regret it—for the service of others. I am a slave of Christ for a foreign people for the unspeakable glory "of eternal life which is in Christ Jesus our Lord."

(11) And if my own people do not know me, "a prophet has no honor in his own country." Perhaps we are not "from one flock" nor have "one God as our father." As Scripture says: "Whoever is not with me is against me, and whoever does not gather with me scatters." It is wrong that "one destroys, another builds up." "I am not seeking what belongs to me." Not my way, but the will of God "who put this care into my heart" so that I would become one "of the hunters and fishermen" whom God long ago promised would come "in the final days."

4. A decurion (Lat. *decurio*) or *curialis*, a member of the local *curia* or town council was an important Roman official for local affairs, especially the collection of taxes (Bowersock 1999, 401 ("Curiales")).

(12) Inuidetur mihi. Quid faciam, Domine? Valde despicior. Ecce oues tuae circa me laniantur atque depraedantur, et supradictis latrunculis, iubente Corotico hostili mente. Longe est a caritate Dei traditor Christianorum in manus Scottorum atque Pictorum. *Lupi rapaces*[af] deglutierunt gregem Domini, qui utique Hiberione cum summa diligentia optime crescebat, et filii Scottorum et filiae regulorum monachi et uirgines Christi enumerare nequeo. Quam ob rem *iniuria iustorum non te placeat*; etiam *usque ad inferos non placebit.*[ag]

(13) Quis sanctorum non horreat iocundare uel conuiuium fruere cum talibus? De spoliis defunctorum Christianorum repleuerunt domos suas, de rapinis uiuunt. Nesciunt miseri uenenum letale cibum porrigunt ad amicos et filios suos, sicut Eua non intellexit quod utique mortem tradidit uiro suo.[ah] Sic sunt omnes qui male agunt: mortem perennem poenam operantur.

(14) Consuetudo Romanorum Gallorum Christianorum: mittunt uiros sanctos idoneos ad Francos et ceteras gentes cum tot milia solidorum ad redimendos captiuos baptizatos. Tu potius interficis et uendis illos genti exterae ignoranti Deum; quasi in lupanar tradis *membra Christi.*[ai] Qualem spem habes in Deum, uel qui te consentit aut qui te communicat uerbis adulationis? Deus iudicabit. Scriptum est enim: *Non solum facientes mala sed etiam consentientes damnandi sunt.*[aj]

(15) Nescio *quid dicam uel quid loquar*[ak] amplius de defunctis filiorum Dei, quos gladius supra modum dure tetigit. Scriptum est enim: *Flete cum flentibus,*[al] et iterum: *Si dolet unum membrum condoleant omnia membra.*[am] Quapropter ecclesia plorat et plangit filios et filias suas quas adhuc gladius nondum interfecit, sed prolongati et exportati in longa terrarum, ubi peccatum manifeste grauiter impudenter abundat, ibi uenundati ingenui homines,

af. Mt 7.15 ag. Sir 9.17 ah. V. Gn 3.6. ai. 1 Cor 6.15
aj. Rom 1.32 ak. V. Jn 12.49. al. Rom 12.15 am. 1Cor 12.26

(12) I am hated. What am I to do, O Lord? I am deeply despised. Look how your sheep all around me are torn to pieces and driven away by these thieves, by the orders of this evil-minded Coroticus. Far from the love of God is anyone who hands over Christians to the Irish and Picts. "Ravaging wolves" have devoured the flock of God, which in Ireland was fast increasing by diligent care. I cannot count how many sons and daughters of Irish kings were becoming monks and virgins of Christ. Therefore "do not let wrongs against the righteous please you—even Hell will not be pleased."

(13) Who of the saints would not shrink from laughing with or attending the dinners of such men? They fill their homes with the spoils of dead Christians and live on plunder. These poor fools do not realize the food they serve to friends and their own children is deadly poison, just as Eve was ignorant that she handed death to her own husband. All who do evil are like this—they are working towards their own punishment of everlasting death.

(14) This is the custom of the Roman Christians in Gaul, that they send holy and capable men to the Franks[5] and other tribes with great bags of money to redeem baptized captives. You, on the other hand, murder Christians and sell them to foreign people who do not know God—as if you handed over "the body of Christ" into a brothel. What hope do you have in God? Who can agree with you or praise you? God will judge. As Scripture says: "Not only those doing evil but even those condoning it will be damned."

(15) I do not know "what to say" or "what more to speak" concerning the slain children of God, those whom the sword has touched so bitterly. It is written: "Weep with those who weep." And again: "If one member of the body mourns, let all mourn." And thus the Church laments and mourns her sons and daughters who have not yet been killed, but have been taken so far away to a distant land where sin abounds so abundantly, grievously, and shamelessly. There

5. The Franks were a Germanic tribe causing frequent trouble for the Romans in the late Empire along the middle and lower Rhine. They converted to Christianity in the late fifth century (see James 1988).

Christiani in seruitute redacti sunt, praesertim indignissimorum pessimorum apostatarumque Pictorum.

(16) Idcirco cum tristitia et maerore uociferabo: O speciosissimi atque amantissimi fratres et filii *quos in Christo genui*[an] enumerare nequeo, quid faciam uobis? Non sum dignus Deo neque hominibus subuenire. *Praeualuit iniquitas iniquorum super nos.*[ao] Quasi *extranei facti sumus.*[ap] Forte non credunt *unum baptismum* percepimus uel *unum Deum patrem*[aq] habemus. Indignum est illis Hiberionaci sumus. Sicut ait: Nonne *unum Deum* habetis? *Quid dereliquistis unusquisque proximum suum?*[ar]

(17) Idcirco doleo pro uobis, doleo, carissimi mihi; sed iterum gaudeo intra meipsum: non gratis laboraui uel peregrinatio mea in uacuum non fuit. Et contigit scelus tam horrendum ineffabile, Deo gratias, creduli baptizati, de saeculo recessistis ad paradisum. Cerno uos: migrare coepistis ubi *nox non erit neque luctus neque mors amplius, sed exultabitis sicut uituli ex uinculis resoluti et conculcabitis iniquos et erunt cinis sub pedibus uestris.*[as]

(18) Vos ergo regnabitis cum apostolis et prophetis atque martyribus. Aeterna regna capietis, sicut ipse testatur inquit: *Venient ab oriente et occidente et recumbent cum Abraham et Isaac et Iacob in regno caelorum.*[at] *Foris canes et uenefici et homicidae,*[au] et: *Mendacibus periuris pars eorum in stagnum ignis aeterni.*[av] Non inmerito ait apostolus: *Vbi iustus uix saluus erit, peccator et impius transgressor legis ubi se recognoscet?*[aw]

(19) Vnde enim Coroticus cum suis sceleratissimis, rebellatores Christi, ubi se uidebunt, qui mulierculas baptizatas praemia distribuunt ob miserum regnum temporale, quod utique in

an. 1 Cor 4.15 ao. Ps 64.4 ap. Ps 68.9 aq. Eph 4.5–6
ar. Mal 2.10. as. Mal 4.2–3 ; cf. Rv 21.4, 22.5. at. Mt 8.11 au. Rv 22.15
av. Rv 21.8 aw. 1Pt 4.18

freeborn people are sold, Christians are made into slaves—slaves of the most abominable, unworthy, apostate Picts!

(16) So I will raise my voice with sadness and grief: O my beautiful and beloved brothers and sons "to whom I gave birth in Christ," so many of you I cannot count—what can I do for you? I am not worthy to help either God or men. "The evils of the wicked have prevailed over us." "We have become," as it were, "strangers." Perhaps they do not believe we have received "one baptism" or that we have "one God, our father." They despise us because we are Irish. But scripture says: "Do you not have one God? Why have you each abandoned your neighbor?"

(17) So I mourn for you, my dearest, I mourn. But I also rejoice within myself. I have not labored in vain nor has my pilgrimage among you been for nothing. And if this horrible, unspeakable crime did have to happen, I thank God that as baptized believers you have departed this world for paradise. I can see you now as you begin your journey to that place where "there is no night, no sorrow, and no more death," but "you will leap like calves released from their ropes. You will grind down the wicked and they will be as ashes under your feet."

(18) You will rule with the apostles, prophets, and martyrs. You will receive an eternal kingdom. For Christ himself has said: "They will come from the east and the west and sit beside Abraham and Isaac and Jacob in the kingdom of heaven." "Outside are dogs and sorcerers, and murderers." Moreover: "Liars and perjurers will have their portion in a lake of everlasting fire." Not without reason does the apostle say: "If the just are scarcely safe, where will the sinner and ungodly transgressor of the law find himself?"

(19) Therefore where will Coroticus and his band of criminals, rebels against Christ, find themselves—men who have distributed baptized women as prizes, all for the sake of this passing world

momento transeat? Sicut nubes uel fumus, qui utique uento dispergitur,[ax] ita peccatores fraudulenti *a facie Domini peribunt;*[ay] *iusti autem epulentur in magna constantia* cum Christo,[az] *iudicabunt nationes et* regibus iniquis *dominabuntur*[ba] *in saecula saeculorum*, Amen.

(20) *Testificor coram Deo et angelis suis*[bb] quod ita erit sicut intimauit imperitiae meae. Non mea uerba sed Dei et apostolorum atque prophetarum quod ego Latinum exposui, qui numquam enim mentiti sunt. *Qui crediderit saluus erit, qui uero non crediderit condempnabitur.*[bc] Deus locutus est.

(21) Quaeso plurimum ut quicumque famulus Dei promptus fuerit ut sit gerulus litterarum harum, ut nequaquam subtrahatur uel abscondatur a nemine, sed magis potius legatur coram cunctis plebibus et praesente ipso Corotico. Quod si Deus inspirat illos ut quandoque Deo resipiscant, ita ut uel sero paeniteant quod tam impie gesserunt—homicida erga fratres Domini—et liberent captiuas baptizatas quas ante ceperunt, ita ut mereantur Deo uiuere et sani efficiantur hic et in aeternum. Pax Patri et Filio et Spiritui Sancto. Amen.

ax. Cf. Wis 5.15. ay. Ps 67.3–4 az. Wis 5.1 ba. Wis 3.8
bb. 1Tm 5.21 bc. Mk 16.16

which will vanish in a moment? "Just like a cloud or smoke blown away by the wind," so these lying sinners "will disappear from the sight of God." "But the just will feast in great confidence with Christ. "They will judge the nations and will rule over" wicked kings forever and ever. Amen.

(20) "I testify before God and his angels" that it will happen as he has revealed to me, ignorant though I am. These are not my words, but those of God and the apostles and prophets, who have never lied, which I write in Latin. "Whoever believes will be saved, whoever does not believe will be condemned." God has spoken.

(21) I ask earnestly anyone who is a servant of God to be a bearer of this letter, so that it not be suppressed or hidden by anyone. But let it be read before all people, even before Coroticus himself. May God inspire them somehow to come to their senses before Him, so that, though late, they might repent of their wicked crimes—these murderers of the brothers of the Lord—and release the baptized captives whom they kidnapped. In this way they might earn the right to live with God and be saved, both here and for eternity. Peace to the Father and the Son and the Holy Spirit. Amen.

CONFESSIO

(1) Ego Patricius peccator rusticissimus et minimus omnium fidelium et contemptibilissimus apud plurimos. Patrem habui Calpornium diaconum filium quendam Potiti presbyteri, qui fuit uico Bannauenta Berniae; uillulam enim prope habuit, ubi ego capturam dedi. Annorum eram tunc fere sedecim. Deum enim uerum ignorabam et Hiberione in captiuiatate adductus sum cum tot milia hominum—secundum merita nostra, quia a Deo recessimus et *praecepta* eius non *custodiuimus*[a] et sacerdotibus nostris non oboedientes fuimus, qui nostram salutem admonebant: et Dominus induxit super nos iram animationis suae[b] et *dispersit* nos *in gentibus*[c] multis etiam *usque ad ultimum terrae*,[d] ubi nunc paruitas mea esse uidetur inter alienigenas.

(2) Et ibi Dominus *aperuit sensum incredulitatis meae*,[e] ut uel sero rememorarem delicta mea et ut *conuerterem toto corde ad Dominum Deum meum*,[f] qui *respexit humilitatem meam*[g] et misertus est adolescentiae et ignorantiae meae et custodiuit me antequam scirem eum et antequam saperem uel distinguerem inter bonum et malum et muniuit me et consolatus est me ut pater filium.

(3) Vnde autem tacere non possum, *neque expedit quidem*,[h] tanta beneficia et tantam gratiam quam mihi Dominus praestare

1.2 *contemptibilissimus*: D contemptibilis sum. **1.4** *Bannauenta Berniae*: AP bennauem taburniae; CRVGF bennauem taburnie.

a. Gn 26.5 b. Cf. Is. 42.25. c. Jer 9.16 d. Acts 1.8
e. Lk 24.45; Heb 3.12 f. Jl 2.12 g. Lk 1.48 h. 2Cor 12.1

ST. PATRICK'S *CONFESSION*

(1) I, Patrick, a sinner, am a most unsophisticated man, the least of all Christians, and to many the most despised. My father was Calpornius,[1] a deacon,[2] who was son of the priest[3] Potitus from the village of Bannaventa Berniae.[4] He had a villa nearby where I was captured when I was about sixteen years old. I was ignorant of the true God then and was led away to Ireland with many thousands of others. We deserved our fate because we had turned away from God and "did not keep his commandments." We did not obey our priests who warned us again and again about our salvation. And the Lord overwhelmed us with the anger of his spirit and "scattered us among many nations" even "to the very ends of the earth" where now my smallness is seen among strangers.

(2) And there the Lord "opened my understanding about my unbelief," so that although late I might remember my sins and "turn my whole heart to the Lord my God," who "looked upon my misery" and had mercy on my youth and ignorance. He watched over me before I knew him, before I had any wisdom, before I could distinguish between good and evil. He protected and comforted me as a father would his son.

(3) Therefore I cannot be silent, "nor indeed is it proper to do so," because of the great benefits and abundant grace the Lord saw fit to

1. The name *Calpornius* (or more commonly *Calpurnius*) is frequent in Roman Britain (e.g. Collingwood and Wright 1965, vol. 1 #155, #320, #1142).

2. The deaconate was a minor order in the early Church with various functions such as lector and keeper of church property. The office was not necessarily a step to ordination to the priesthood as it was for Patrick (*Conf.* .27).

3. The office of priest (Lat. *presbyter*) did not exclude marriage.

4. Patrick's home is recorded in the manuscripts as *bannauem tabernia*(*e*), but this form of the name makes no sense in either Latin or British Celtic. As *Bannaventa* occurs elsewhere in Roman Britain as a town name, the best reading is the same name further designated by *Berniae* (perhaps "of the mountain pass"). See Rivet and Smith 1979, 511–12.

dignatus est *in terra captiuitatis meae;*[i] quia haec est retributio nostra, ut post correptionem uel agnitionem Dei *exaltare et confiteri mirabilia eius*[j] coram *omni natione quae est sub omni caelo.*[k]

(4) Quia non est alius Deus nec umquam fuit nec ante nec erit post haec praeter Deum Patrem ingenitum, sine principio, a quo est omne principium, omnia tenetem, ut didicimus; et huius filium Iesum Christum, quem cum Patre scilicet semper fuisse testamur, ante originem saeculi spiritaliter apud Patrem inenarrabiliter genitum ante omne principium, et per ipsum facta sunt uisibilia et inuisibilia, hominem factum, morte deuicta in caelis ad Patrem receptum, *et dedit illi omnem potestatem super omne nomen caelestium et terrestrium et infernorum et omnis lingua confiteatur ei quia Dominus* et Deus *est Iesus Christus,*[l] quem credimus et expectamus aduentum ipsius mox futurum, *iudex uiuorum atque mortuorum,* [m] *qui reddet unicuique secundum facta sua;*[n] et *effudit in nobis habunde Spiritum Sanctum,*[o] donum et pignus inmortalitatis, qui facit credentes et oboedientes ut sint *filii Dei* et *coheredes Christi:*[p] quem confitemur et adoramus unum Deum in trinitate sacri nominis.

(5) Ipse enim dixit per prophetam: *Inuoca me in die tribulationis tuae et liberabo te et magnificabis me.*[q] Et iterum inquit: *Opera autem Dei reuelare et confiteri honorificum est.*[r]

(6) Tamen etsi in multis imperfectus sum opto fratribus et cognatis meis scire qualitatem meam, ut possint perspicere uotum animae meae.

(7) Non ignoro *testimonium Domini mei,*[s] qui in psalmo testatur: *Perdes eos qui loquuntur mendacium.*[t] Et iterum inquit: *Os*

i. 2Chr 6.37 j. Is 25.1 ; Ps. 88.6 k. Acts 2.5 l. Phil 2.9–11
m. Acts 10.42 n. Rom 2.6 o. Ti 3.6 p. Cf. Rom 8.17.
q. Ps 49.15 r. Tb 12.7 s. 2Tm 1.8 t. Ps 6.7

grant me "in the land of my captivity." This is how we return thanks to him, so that after he corrects us and we turn to him, "we exalt him and praise his wonders" before "every nation under heaven."

(4) For there is no other God nor was there ever before or after except God the uncreated Father. He is without beginning, but in him all things have their beginning. He is, as we say, the one who holds everything together. Jesus Christ is his Son, whom we declare was always present with the Father, spiritually begotten by the Father from before the beginning of the world, before the beginning of anything, though how this happened is beyond words. Through him all things were made, visible and invisible. He became a human being, and having conquered death, was taken back to heaven by the Father. "And God gave him all power above every name in heaven and on earth and under the earth, so that every tongue may confess that Jesus Christ is Lord" and God. We believe in him and expect him to return soon as "judge of the living and the dead." "He will repay each person according to their actions." "He has abundantly poured on us the Holy Spirit," the gift and pledge of immortality, who makes those who believe and obey into "children of God" and "fellows heirs of Christ." This is the God we believe in and adore—one God in the Trinity of the sacred name.

(5) As he himself said through the prophet: "Call on me in your day of trouble and I will deliver you and you will glorify me." And again he says: "It is honorable to reveal and confess the works of God."

(6) Although I am imperfect in many ways I want my brothers and family to know what kind of person I am, so that they might understand the desire of my heart.

(7) I am not forgetting "the testimony of my Lord," who in the Psalm declares: "You will destroy those who speak lies." And again

quod mentitur occidit animam.[u] Et idem Dominus in euangelio inquit: *Verbum otiosum quod locuti fuerint homines reddent pro eo rationem in die iudicii.*[v]

(8) Vnde autem uehementer debueram *cum timore et tremore*[w] metuere hanc sententiam in die illa ubi nemo se poterit subtrahere uel abscondere, sed omnes omnino *reddituri sumus rationem*[x] etiam minimorum peccatorum *ante tribunal Domini Christi.*[y]

(9) Quapropter olim cogitaui scribere, sed et usque nunc haesitaui; timui enim ne incederem in linguam hominum, quia non didici sicut et ceteri, qui optime itaque iura et sacras litteras utraque pari modo combiberunt et sermones illorum ex infantia numquam mutarunt, sed magis ad perfectum semper addiderunt. Nam sermo et loquela nostra translata est in linguam alienam, sicut facile potest probari ex saliua scripturae meae qualiter sum ego in sermonibus instructus atque eruditus, quia, inquit, *sapiens per linguam dinoscetur et sensus et scientia et doctrina ueritatis.*[z]

(10) Sed quid prodest excusatio iuxta ueritatem, praesertim cum praesumptione, quatenus modo ipse adpeto in senectute mea quod in iuuentute non comparui? quod obstiterunt peccata mea ut confirmarem quod ante perlegeram. Sed quis me credit etsi dixero quod ante praefatus sum? Adolescens, immo paene puer inuerbis, capturam dedi, antequam scirem quid adpetere uel quid uitare debueram. Vnde ergo hodie erubesco et uehementer pertimeo denudare imperitiam meam, quia desertis breuitate sermone explicare nequeo, sicut enim spiritus gestit et animus, et sensus monstrat adfectus.

(11) Sed si itaque datum mihi fuisset sicut et ceteris, uerumtamen non silerem *propter retributionem,*[aa] et si forte uidetur apud aliquantos me in hoc praeponere cum mea inscientia et *tardiori lingua,*[ab] sed etiam scriptum est enim: *Linguae balbutientes uelociter discent loqui pacem.*[ac] Quanto magis nos adpetere

u. Wis 1.11 v. Mt 12.36 w. Eph 6.5 et 2Cor 7.15 x. Rom 14.12
y. Rom 14.10 z. Sir 4.29 aa. Ps 118.112 ab. Ex 4.10
ac. Is 32.4

he says: "the lying mouth destroys the soul." And again the Lord says in the Gospel: "On the day of judgment everyone will give an account of each idle word they have spoken."

(8) Therefore I ought to dread this sentence "with fear and trembling" on that day when no one will be able to escape or hide, but "all of us will give an account" of everything, even the smallest of sins, "before the judgment seat of the Lord Christ."

(9) Because of this I have long thought of writing this account, but I hesitated until now. I was afraid I would be criticized since I was not educated like others who have studied both law and theology in equal measure. Such men have not had to change their speech since childhood, but have instead continually perfected it. I, on the other hand, have had to speak in a foreign language.[5] You can easily see from my writing just what kind of instruction and training I have had. As it is written: "A wise man is known through his speech, as is understanding and knowledge and the teaching of truth."

(10) But what use is an excuse however true, since it is presumptuous for me as an old man to wish for something I failed to acquire in my youth? My sins then prevented me from truly learning what I had read. But who will believe me even if I repeat what I said before? I was just a young man, almost a speechless boy, when I was captured, scarcely knowing what I ought to seek or avoid. This is why today I am embarrassed and greatly fear to reveal my lack of education. I am not able to explain myself clearly as my spirit and mind long to do so that my words might match my feelings.

(11) But if I had been given the same opportunity as others, then "for the sake of reward" I would certainly not be silent. And if seems to some that I am arrogant for speaking in spite of my ignorance and "slow tongue," remember that it is written: "Stammering tongues will quickly learn to speak peace." How much more we

5. Patrick was a native speaker of British, a Celtic tongue ancestral to Welsh. He would have learned Latin as a boy, then Irish (also a Celtic language) as a captive and used it during his ministry in Ireland.

debemus, qui sumus, inquit, *epistola Christi in salutem usque ad ultimum terrae,* [ad] et si non deserta, sed ratum et fortissimum *scripta in cordibus uestris non atramento sed spiritu Dei uiui.*[ae] Et iterum Spiritus testatur *et rusticationem ab Altissimo creatam.*[af]

(12) Vnde ego primus rusticus profuga indoctus scilicet, *qui nescio in posterum prouidere,*[ag] sed illud scio certissime quia utique *priusquam humiliarer*[ah] ego eram uelut lapis qui iacet in luto profundo: et uenit *qui potens est*[ai] et in sua misericordia sustulit me et quidem scilicet sursum adleuauit et collocauit me in summo pariete; et inde fortiter debueram exclamare ad retribuendum quoque aliquid Domino pro tantis beneficiis eius hic et in aeternum, quae mens hominum aestimare non potest.

(13) Vnde autem ammiramini itaque *magni et pusilli qui timetis Deum*[aj] et uos dominicati rethorici audite et scrutamini. Quis me stultum excitauit de medio eorum qui uidentur esse sapientes et *legis periti* et *potentes in sermone*[ak] et in omni re, et me quidem, detestabilis huius mundi, prae ceteris inspirauit si talis essem—dummodo autem—ut *cum metu et reuerentia*[al] et sine querella fideliter prodessem genti ad quam caritas Christi transtulit et donauit me in uita mea, si dignus fuero, denique ut cum humilitate et ueraciter deseruirem illis.

(14) In mensura itaque fidei Trinitatis oportet distinguere, sine reprehensione periculi notum facere donum Dei et consulationem aeternam, sine timore fiducialiter Dei nomen ubique expandere, ut etiam post obitum meum exagallias relinquere fratibus et filiis meis quos in Domino ego baptizaui, tot milia hominum.

(15) Et non eram dignus neque talis ut hoc Dominus seruulo suo concederet post aerumnas et tantas moles, post captiuitatem, post annos multos, in gentem illam tantam gratiam mihi donaret, quod ego aliquando in iuuentute mea numquam speraui neque cogitaui.

ad. 2Cor 3.2; Acts 13.47
ae. 2Cor 3.2–3
af. Sir 7.16
ag. Eccl 4.13
ah. Ps 118.67
ai. Lk 1.49
aj. Rv 19.5
ak. Lk 7.30; Lk 24.19
al. Heb 12.28

should desire this, we who are, as it says, "the letter of Christ for salvation to the end of the earth." And though not an elegant letter, I am determined, "written in your hearts not with ink but with the spirit of the living God." And again the Spirit says: "Even the rustic man was created by the Most High."

(12) So at first I was a rustic, an ignorant exile, "who did not know how to provide for the future." But this I know without a doubt—"before I was humbled" I was like a stone lying in deep mud. Then "he who is powerful" in his mercy lifted me up, raised me on high, and placed me on top of a wall. This is why I must proclaim with all my might and give thanks to the Lord for all his marvelous blessings, now and forever more—blessings beyond all human imagination.

(13) So be amazed "you both great and small who fear God"—you wealthy and learned men—listen and consider this. Who raised up foolish me from among you, you who seem to be wise, "learned in the law," "powerful in speech" and in every other way? Indeed God inspired me, despised in this world, ahead of others to serve faithfully throughout my life—if only I could—"with fear and reverence" the people to whom Christ's love brought and dedicated me, if I might be worthy to truly serve them with humility.

(14) Because of my faith in the Trinity I must make known the gift of God and his eternal consolation without worry about any dangers. I must faithfully spread the name of God everywhere, so that after my death I leave a legacy for my brothers and sons whom I baptized in the Lord, so many thousands of people.

(15) I was not at all worthy of what the Lord was to grant to his servant after misfortunes and such great difficulties, after captivity, after so many years—he gave such grace to me for the sake of these people. I never hoped for such a thing or even thought of it in my youth.

(16) Sed postquam Hiberione deueneram, cotidie itaque pecora pascebam et frequens in die orabam, magis ac magis accedebat amor Dei et timor ipsius et fides augebatur et spiritus agebatur, ut in die una usque ad centum orationes et in nocte prope similiter, ut etiam in siluis et monte manebam, et ante lucem excitabar ad orationem per niuem per gelu per pluuiam, et nihil mali sentiebam neque ulla pigritia erat in me. Sicut modo uideo, quia tunc spiritus in me feruebat.

(17) et ibi scilicet quadam nocte in somno audiui uocem dicentem mihi: "Bene ieiunas cito iturus ad patriam tuam." Et iterum post paululum tempus audiui responsum dicentem mihi: "Ecce nauis tua parata est"—et non erat prope, sed forte habebat ducenta milia passus et ibi numquam fueram nec ibi notum quemquam de hominibus habebam—et deinde postmodum conuersus sum in fugam et intermisi hominem cum quo fueram sex annis et ueni in uirtute Dei, qui uiam meam ad bonum dirigebat et nihil metuebam donec perueni ad nauem illam.

(18) Et illa die qua perueni profecta est nauis de loco suo, et locutus sum ut haberem unde nauigare cum illis et gubernator displicuit illi et acriter cum indignatione respondit: "Nequaquam tu nobiscum adpetes ire," et cum haec audiissem separaui me ab illis ut uenirem ad tegoriolum ubi hospitabam, et in itinere coepi orare et antequam orationem consummarem audiui unum ex illis et fortiter exclamabat post me: "Veni cito, quia uocant te homines isti," et statim ad illos reuersus sum, et coeperunt mihi dicere: "Veni, quia ex fide recipimus te. Fac nobiscum amicitiam quo modo uolueris." et in illa die itaque reppuli sugere mammellas eorum propter timorem Dei, sed uerumtamen ab illis speraui uenire in fidem Iesu Christi, quia gentes erant. et ob hoc obtinui cum illis, et protinus nauigauimus.

18.137–8 *sugere mammellas eorum*: P fugere manus illorum; RF fugire mammas illorum.

(16) But after I came to Ireland I tended sheep every day and prayed frequently. More and more my love for God grew and my fear of him, as my faith and spirit increased. In one day I would pray up to a hundred times and the same at night, even when I was in the woods on the mountain. I rose before dawn to pray through snow, cold, or rain. I suffered no harm from it nor was there any laziness in me. I can see now that the spirit was burning within me.

(17) It was there one night while I was sleeping that I heard a voice say to me: "You have fasted well. Soon you will return to your homeland." Soon after I again heard a voice saying to me: "Behold, your ship is ready." But the ship was not nearby, but in a place perhaps two hundred miles away.[6] I had never been there nor did I know anyone there. But soon after I fled and left the man I had served for six years. I traveled with courage from God, who guided my way towards good. I feared nothing until I arrived at the ship.

(18) And on the day I arrived the ship was about to depart from that place. I asked if I might sail with them, but the captain was indignant and answered harshly: "There is no way you are coming with us!" When I heard this I left and went back towards the hut where I was staying, praying on the way. But before my prayer was finished one of the sailors was shouting loudly at me: "Come back quickly! These men want to talk with you." Immediately I returned and they said to me: "Come, we'll take you on faith. Make a pact of friendship with us however you wish." But on that day I refused to suck their breasts[7] because I feared God. Nevertheless I hoped they would come to a faith in Jesus Christ since they were pagans. Thus I had my way and we set out immediately.

6. 200 Roman miles is roughly 185 statute miles or 300 kilometers.

7. The phrase *sugere mammellas eorum* has troubled editors and readers for centuries. To suck on another's breast is in fact a symbolic act of adoption found in a number of cultures, including early Ireland. See Maier 1999. The phrase also echoes Is. 60.16.

(19) Et post triduum terram cepimus et uiginti octo dies per desertum iter fecimus et cibus defuit illis et fames inualuit super eos, et alio die coepit gubernator mihi dicere: "Quid est, Christiane? Tu dicis deus tuus magnus et omnipotens est, quare ergo non potes pro nobis orare? Quia nos a fame periclitamur; difficle est enim ut aliquem hominem umquam uideamus." Ego enim confidenter dixi illis: "*Conuertimini* ex fide *ex toto corde ad Dominum Deum meum,*[am] quia nihil est impossibile illi, ut hodie cibum mittat uobis in uiam uestram usque dum satiamini, quia ubique habundat illi," et adiuuante Deo ita factum est. Ecce grex porcorum in uia ante oculos nostros apparuit, et multos ex illis interfecerunt et ibi duas noctes manserunt et bene refecti et canes eorum repleti sunt, quia multi ex illis defecerunt et secus uiam semiuiui relicti sunt. Et post hoc summas gratias egerunt Deo et ego honorificatus sum sub oculis eorum, et ex hac die cibum habundanter habuerunt; etiam mel siluestre inuenerunt et mihi partem obtulerunt et unus ex illis dixit: "Immolaticium est." Deo gratias, exinde nihil gustaui.

(20) Eadem uero nocte eram dormiens et fortiter temptauit me satanas, quod memor ero *quamdiu fuero in hoc corpore,*[an] et cecidit super me uelut saxum ingens et nihil membrorum meorum praeualens. Sed unde me uenit ignaro in spiritu ut Heliam uocarem? Et inter haec uidi in caelum solem oriri et dum clamarem "Helia, Helia" uiribus meis, ecce splendor solis illius decidit super me et statim discussit a me omnem grauitudinem, et credo quod a Christo Domino meo subuentus sum et Spiritus eius iam tunc clamabat pro me et spero quod sic erit *in die pressurae* meae,[ao] sicut in euangelio inquit: *In illa die*, Dominus testatur, *non uos estis qui loquimini, sed Spiritus Patris uestri qui loquitur in uobis.*[ap]

19.152–3 *canes eorum repleti*: P carnes eorum releuati. **20.2** *fuero*: RFCG fueram.

am. Jl 2.12 an. 2Pet 1.13 ao. Ps 58.17, 76.3, 85.7. ap. Mt 10.19–20

(19) After three days we made landfall and wandered through an empty region for twenty-eight days. They had no food and were overcome by hunger, so that on the next day the captain said to me: "Tell me, Christian, you say your god is so great and powerful, why are you powerless to pray for us? We are worn away by hunger and it is unlikely we will ever see another human being again." But I said to them full of confidence: "Turn your hearts in faith to the Lord my God, because nothing is impossible to him. From his abundance he may send food to you today on your journey so that you will be satisfied." And with God's help, that's just what happened. A great herd of pigs appeared before their eyes on the road, so that they killed many of them and were well fed, remaining there for two nights. Even their dogs were satisfied,[8] as many of them had grown weak and were only half alive at that point. After this they gave thanks to God and I was honored in their eyes, since from that day they had abundant food. They even found some wild honey and gave me part of it, one of them saying, "This has been offered as a sacrifice." Thanks be to God I had eaten none of it.

(20) On that same night while I was sleeping, Satan strongly tempted me. I will remember it "as long as I am in this body." Something like a huge rock fell on me so that I could not move any of my limbs. But how did it occur to me, ignorant in spiritual matters, to call on Elijah? Just at this point I saw the sun rising in the sky so that I called out, "Elijah, Elijah" with all my might.[9] Behold the rays of the sun fell on me and immediately took away the weight on my limbs. I believe that it was Christ Jesus helping me and his Spirit crying out through me. So I hope it will be "on the day of my distress." As the gospel says, "On that day," the Lord declares, "it is not you who speaks but the Spirit of your Father who speaks in you."

8. Large dogs were a noted export from Ireland to the Roman world (Quintus Aurelius Symmachus *Letter* 2.77).

9. In early Christian tradition and iconography, the prophet Elijah (Lat. *Helias*) was sometimes fused with the Greek sun-god of similar name (Lat. *Helios*) especially as Elijah was carried into the heavens in a fiery chariot (2Kgs 2.11).

(21) Et iterum post annos multos adhuc capturam dedi. Ea nocte prima itaque mansi cum illis, responsum autem diuinum audiui dicentem mihi: "Duobus mensibus eris cum illis." Quod ita factum est: nocte illa sexagesima *liberauit me Dominus de manibus eorum.*[aq]

(22) Etiam in itinere praeuidit nobis cibum et ignem et siccitatem cotidie donec decimo die peruenimus homines. Sicut superius insinuaui, uiginti et octo dies per desertum iter fecimus et ea nocte qua peruenimus homines de cibo uero nihil habuimus.

(23) Et iterum post paucos annos in Britanniis eram cum parentibus meis, qui me ut filium susceperunt et ex fide rogauerunt me ut uel modo ego post tantas tribulationes quas ego pertuli nusquam ab illis discederem, et ibi scilicet *uidi in uisu noctis*[ar] uirum uenientem quasi de Hiberione, cui nomen Victoricus, cum epistolis innumerabilibus, et dedit mihi unam ex his et legi principium epistolae continentem "Vox Hiberionacum," et cum recitabam principium epistolae putabam ipso momento audire uocem ipsorum, qui erant iuxta siluam Vocluti quae est prope mare occidentale, et sic exclamauerunt *quasi ex uno ore:*[as] "Rogamus te, sancte puer, ut uenias et adhuc ambulas inter nos," et ualde *compunctus sum corde*[at] et amplius non potui legere et sic expertus sum. Deo gratias, quia post plurimus annos praestitit illis Dominus secundum clamorem illorum.

(24) Et alia nocte—*nescio, Deus scit,*[au] utrum in me an iuxta me—uerbis pertissime, quos ego audiui et non potui intellegere, nisi ad postremum orationis sic effitiatus est: "Qui dedit animam suam pro te, ipse est qui loquitur in te," et sic expertus sum gaudibundus.

23.187 *Vocluti*: D Focluti.

aq. Gn 37.21 ar. Dn 7.13 as. Dn 3.51 at. Ps 108.17
au. 2Cor 12.2

(21) And after many years I was again captured. On the first night I was with them I heard a divine voice speaking to me saying, "For two months you will be with them." That is exactly what happened. On the sixtieth night "the Lord liberated me from their hands."

(22) But on this journey God looked after us with food, fire, and dry weather each day until on the tenth day we reached a settlement. As I said above, we traveled through an empty region for twenty-eight days. We ran out of food on the very night we arrived at the settlement.

(23) And after a few years I was again with my parents in Britain. They welcomed me as a son and begged me, after all the tribulations I had been through, that I would never leave them again. It was there that "I saw a vision in the night" of a man coming as if from Ireland. His name was Victoricus and he carried countless letters.[10] He gave me one of them and I read the opening words which said: "the Voice of the Irish." While I was reading this I thought I heard a voice of those who dwell beside the wood of Voclut near the western sea.[11] It was as if they were exclaiming "with a single voice:" "We beg you, holy boy, come and walk among us again." Truly "I was pierced in my heart" and could read no more, then I woke up. Thanks be to God that after many years the Lord granted them their request.

(24) And on another night—whether within me or near me, "I don't know, God knows"—there were eloquent words which I heard but could not understand, except those at the end: "He who gave his life for you, he himself speaks in you." And I awoke full of joy.

10. Victoricus is a Roman rather than Irish name, so that if Patrick is referring to a real person, the speaker may be a fellow Roman slave he knew during his captivity in Ireland. There may also be a connection to St. Victoricus, a third-century martyr who died preaching in Roman Gaul.

11. The location of Voclut and the original form of the name is controversial, though Tírechán (14) places it near Killala Bay in County Mayo. See Concannon 1940.

(25) Et iterum uidi in me ipsum orantem et eram quasi intra corpus meum et audiui super me, hoc est super *interiorem hominem*,[av] et ibi fortiter orabat gemitibus, et inter haec stupebam et ammirabam et cogitabam quis esset qui in me orabat, sed ad postremum orationis sic effitiatus est ut sit Spiritus, et sic expertus sum et recordatus sum apostolo dicente: *Spiritus adiuuat infirmitates orationis nostrae: nam quod oremus sicut oportet nescimus: sed ipse Spiritus postulat pro nobis gemitibus inenarrabilibus, quae uerbis exprimi non possunt*;[aw] et iterum: *Dominus aduocatus noster postulat pro nobis.*[ax]

(26) Et quando temptatus sum ab aliquantis senioribus meis, qui uenerunt, et peccata mea, contra laboriosum episcopatum meum, utique illo die fortiter *impulsus sum ut caderem*[ay] hic et in aeternum; sed Dominus pepercit proselito et peregrino propter nomen suum benigne et ualde mihi subuenit in hac conculcatione. Quod in labe et in obprobrium non male deueni. Deum oro ut *non illis in peccatum reputetur.*[az]

(27) *Occasionem* post annos triginta *inuenerunt me aduersus*[ba] uerbum quod confessus fueram antequam essem diaconus. Propter anxietatem maesto animo insinuaui amicissimo meo quae in pueritia mea una die gesseram, immo in una hora, quia necdum praeualebam. *Nescio, Deus scit,*[bb] si habebam tunc annos quindecim, et Deum uiuum non credebam, neque ex infantia mea, sed in morte et in incredulitate mansi donec ualde castigatus sum *et in ueritate humilitatus sum a fame et nuditate*,[bc] et cotidie.

(28) Contra, Hiberione non sponte pergebam, donec prope deficiebam; sed hoc potius bene mihi fuit, qui ex hoc emendatus sum a Domino, et aptauit me ut hodie essem quod aliquando longe a me erat, ut ego curam haberem aut satagerem pro salute aliorum, quando autem tunc etiam de me ipso non cogitabam.

av. Eph 3.16
aw. Rom 8.26
ax. 1Jn 2.1
ay. Ps 117.13
az. 2Tm 4.16
ba. Dn 6.5
bb. 2Cor 12.2
bc. 2Cor 11.27; Dt 28.48

(25) At another time I saw someone praying within me as if I were inside my own body. I heard him praying above me, that is, above "the inner man," and he was praying powerfully with sighs. All through this I was mystified and astonished and wondered who it was who was praying inside me. But at the end of the prayer he said that he was the Spirit. Then I woke up and remembered what the apostle said: "The Spirit helps the weakness in our prayers. For we do not know what we should pray for, but the Spirit himself prays for us with unspeakable sighs that cannot be expressed in words." And again: "The Lord our advocate speaks for us."

(26) And when I was accused by some of my superiors who came forward and charged me with sins contrary to my laborious episcopate, on that day strongly "I was struck down and might have fallen" in this life and for eternity. But then the Lord kindly spared a stranger and pilgrim on account of his name and helped me mightily in my affliction, so that I did not slip badly into shame and infamy. I pray that God "does not hold this sin against them."

(27) "The charge they brought against me" after thirty years was due to a confession I had made before I was even a deacon. When I was anxious and worried I told my best friend about something I had done in my youth one day, even in one hour, because I was then still weak. "I don't know, God knows," perhaps I was only fifteen years old at the time and did not believe in the living God—I hadn't since childhood—but I remained in death and unbelief until I was severely punished, "and truly brought low by hunger and nakedness" every day.

(28) To the contrary, I did not go to Ireland of my own free will. Indeed, I almost died there. But it turned out well for me since I was chastised by the Lord. He made me what I am today—someone far different than I was then—so that I might work for the care and salvation of others. At that earlier time I did not even care about myself.

(29) Igitur in illo die quo reprobatus sum a memoratis superdictis ad noctem illam *uidi in uisu noctis*[bd] scriptum erat contra faciem meam sine honore, et inter haec audiui responsum diuinum dicentem mihi: "Male uidimus faciem designati nudato nomine." Nec sic praedixit: "Male uidisti," sed: "Male uidimus," quasi sibi se iunxisset, sicut dixit: *Qui uos tangit quasi qui tangit pupillam oculi meam.*[be]

(30) Idcirco *gratias ago ei qui me* in omnibus *confortauit,*[bf] ut non me impediret a profectione quam statueram et de mea quoque opera quod a Christo Domino meo didiceram, sed magis ex eo sensi in me uirtutem non paruam et *fides mea probata est coram Deo et hominibus.*[bg]

(31) Vnde autem *audenter dico*[bh] non me reprehendit conscientia mea hic et in futurum: *teste Deo*[bi] habeo quia non sum mentitus in sermonibus quos ego retuli uobis.

(32) Sed magis doleo pro amicissimo meo cur hoc meruimus audire tale responsum, cui ego credidi etiam animam. Et comperi ab aliquantis fratribus ante defensionem illam—quod ego non interfui nec in Brittanniis eram nec a me oriebatur—ut et ille in mea absentia pulsaret pro me; etiam mihi ipse ore suo dixerat: "Ecce dandus es tu ad gradum episcopatus," quod non eram dignus. Sed unde uenit illi postmodum ut coram cunctis, bonis et malis, et me publice dehonestaret quod ante sponte et laetus indulserat, et Dominus, qui maior omnibus est?

(33) Satis dico. Sed tamen non debeo abscondere donum Dei quod largitus est nobis in terra captiuitatis meae, quia tunc fortiter inquisiui eum et ibi inueni illum et seruauit me ab omnibus iniquitatibus, sic credo, propter inhabitantem Spiritum eius, qui operatus est usque in hanc diem in me. Audenter rursus. Sed scit Deus, si mihi homo hoc effatus fuisset, forsitan tacuissem propter caritatem Christi.

bd. Dn 7.13 be. Zec 2.8 bf. 1Tim 1.12 bg. Sir 25.1
bh. Acts 2.29 bi. Rom 1.9

(29) On the day I was rejected by those mentioned above, "I saw a vision of the night" that same evening. There was disrespectful writing opposite my face, and at once I heard a divine voice saying to me: "We have seen with anger the face of our chosen one stripped of honor." Note that he did not say, "You have seen with anger," but "We have seen with anger," as if he were joined to me. As it says: "Whoever touches you touches the pupil of my eye."

(30) Therefore "I give thanks to him who comforts me" in all things as he did not hinder me in my chosen journey and in the work which I had learned from Christ the Lord. But instead I felt in myself a great strength and that "my faith was proven before God and men."

(31) And so "I boldly declare" my conscience is clear now and in the future. "God is my witness" that I have not lied in those things I have told you.

(32) But I am very sorry for my dearest friend, to whom I trusted my very soul, that we had to hear such words. I learned from some of the brothers before the defense—I was not present at it, nor was I in Britain, nor did I request it—that he spoke up for me in my absence. He was even the one who told me with his own lips: "Behold, you are going to be given the rank of bishop"—even though I was not worthy. But why afterwards did he publicly disgrace me in front of everyone, good and bad, about something about which he had earlier happily and freely pardoned me, as has the Lord who is greater than everyone?

(33) I have said enough. But I must not hide the gift of God which he has given me in the land of my captivity, because I earnestly sought him and there I found him and he saved me from all evil. I believe this because of his Spirit living inside me who has worked in me to this very day. Again I speak boldly. But God knows that if a man had said this to me perhaps I would have remained quiet because of Christ's love.

(34) Vnde ergo indefessam gratiam ago Deo meo, qui me fidelem seruauit *in die temptationis* meae,[bj] ita ut hodie confidenter offeram illi sacrificium ut *hostiam uiuentem*[bk] animam meam Christo Domino meo, qui me *seruauit ab omnibus angustiis meis,*[bl] ut et dicam: *Quis ego sum, Domine,*[bm] uel quae est uocatio mea, qui mihi tanta diuinitate cooperasti, ita ut hodie in gentibus constanter exaltarem et magnificarem nomen tuum ubicumque loco fuero, nec non in secundis sed etiam in pressuris, ut quicquid mihi euenerit siue bonum siue malum aequaliter debeo suscipere et Deo gratias semper agere, qui mihi ostendit ut indubitabilem eum sine fine crederem et qui me audierit ut ego inscius et *in nouissimis diebus*[bn] hoc opus tam pium et tam mirificum auderem adgredere, ita ut imitarem quippiam illos quos ante Dominus iam olim praedixerat praenuntiaturos euangelium suum *in testimonium omnibus gentibus* ante *finem mundi,*[bo] quod ita ergo uidimus itaque suppletum est: ecce testes sumus quia euangelium praedicatum est usque ubi nemo ultra est.

(35) Longum est autem totum per singula enarrare laborem meum uel per partes. Breuiter dicam qualiter piissimus Deus de seruitute saepe liberauit et de periculis duodecim qua periclitata est anima mea, praeter insidias multas et quae uerbis exprimere non ualeo. Nec iniuriam legentibus faciam; sed Deum auctorem habeo, qui nouit omnia etiam antequam fiant, ut me pauperculum pupillum ideo tamen responsum diuinum creber admonere.

(36) *Vnde mihi haec sapientia,*[bp] quae in me non erat, qui nec *numerum dierum noueram*[bq] neque Deum sapiebam? Vnde mihi postmodum donum tam magnam tam salubre Deum agnoscere uel diligere, sed ut patriam et parentes amitterem?

(37) Et munera multa mihi offerebantur cum fletu et lacrimis et offendi illos, nec non contra uotum aliquantis de senioribus meis, sed gubernante Deo nullo modo consensi neque adquieui illis—non mea gratia, sed Deus qui uincit in me et resistit illis

bj. Ps 94.9 bk. Rom 12.1 bl. Ps. 33.5 bm. 2Sm 7.18
bn. Acts 2.17 bo. Mt 24.14 bp. Mt 13.54 bq. Ps 38.5

(34) And so I give thanks to my God who preserved his faithful one "in the day of my temptation" so that now I can offer a sacrifice to him, the "living sacrifice" of my soul to Christ my Lord. He "saved me in all my troubles" so that I can say, "who am I, Lord?" and what is my calling? You helped me with such divine power that now I can constantly praise and glorify your name wherever I may be, both in success and failure. Whatever happens to me, whether good or bad, I must always gives thanks to God who has shown me I can trust in him without limit. He is the one who heard me, an ignorant man, "in these last days" so that I might dare to take up this most noble and holy work. I am like those whom the Lord foretold what was to come when his gospel would be preached "as a testimony to all nations before the end of the world." Indeed we now seen these words fulfilled. Behold, we are witnesses that the gospel has been preached to the edge of the inhabited world.

(35) It would take a long time to narrate the story of my work either in whole or in part. So I will simply say that God most merciful often freed me from slavery and from twelve dangers which threatened my life. Aside from these there were many other treacheries I am unable to detail, for I do not wish to bore my readers. But I have as my witness that God, who knows all things before they happen, frequently warned me, wretch that I am, through divine revelations.

(36) "From where did this wisdom come?" It was not from me, who did not "know the number of my days" nor understood God. Where did I get that great, health-giving gift that I might know and love God, although I had to leave my parents and homeland?

(37) Many gifts were offered to me with weeping and tears—and I offended the givers against the wishes of some of my superiors. But with God guiding me I would not agree with them or consent in any way. It was not by my grace but God who resists them all, so

omnibus, ut ego ueneram ad Hibernas gentes euangelium praedicare et ab incredulis contumelias perferre, ut *audirem obprobium peregrinationis meae,*[br] et persecutiones multas usque ad uincula et ut darem ingenuitatem meam pro utilitate aliorm et, si dignus fuero, promptus sum ut etiam animam meam incunctanter et libentissime pro nomine eius et ibi opto impendere eam usque ad mortem, si Dominus mihi indulgeret.

(38) quia ualde debitor sum Deo, qui mihi tantam gratiam donauit ut populi multi per me in Deum renascerentur et postmodum consummarentur et ut clerici ubique illis ordinarentur ad plebem nuper uenientem ad credulitatem, quam sumpsit Dominus ab extremis terrae, sicut olim promiserat per prophetas suos: *Ad te gentes uenient ab extremis terrae et dicent: sicut falsa comparauerunt patres nostri idola et non est in eis utilitas;*[bs] et iterum: *Posui te lumen in gentibus ut sis in salutem usque ad extremum terrae.*[bt]

(39) Et ibi uolo *expectare promissum*[bu] ipsius, qui utique numquam fallit, sicut in euangelio pollicetur: *Venient ab oriente et occidente et recumbent cum Abraam et Isaac et Iacob,*[bv] sicut credimus ab omni mundo uenturi sunt credentes.

(40) Idcirco itaque oportet quidem bene et diligenter piscare, sicut Dominus praemonet et docet dicens: *Venite post me et faciam uos fieri piscatores hominum;*[bw] et iterum dicit per prophetas: *Ecce mitto piscatores et uenatores multos, dicit Deus,*[bx] et cetera. Vnde autem ualde oportebat retia nostra tendere, ita ut *multitudo copiosa et turba*[by] Deo caperetur et ubique essent clerici qui baptizarent et exhortarent populum indigentem et desiderantem, sicut Dominus inquit in euangelio, ammonet et docet dicens: *Euntes ergo nunc docete omnes gentes baptizantes eas in nomine Patris et Filii et Spiritus Sancti docentes eos obseruare omnia quaecumque mandaui uobis: et ecce ego uobiscum sum omnibus diebus*

br. Sir 29.30 bs. Jer 16.19 bt. Acts 13.47 bu. Acts 1.4
bv. Mt 8.11 bw. Mt 4.19 bx. Jer 16.16 by. Lk 6.17

that I might come to the Irish people to preach the gospel and suffer insults from unbelievers. In this way "I might hear reproach because of my wanderings" and suffer many persecutions including chains, while I sacrifice my free birth for the good of others. If I am worthy, I am ready to give up my life willingly and without hesitation for the sake of his name. It is there I wish to live out my life to the end, if the Lord will grant my wish.

(38) For I am very much a debtor to God, who gave me such grace that many people have been reborn in God and later brought to completion. Clerics also have been ordained for these people just now coming to the faith, whom the Lord has brought to himself from the ends of the earth. As he said through his prophets: "The gentiles shall come to you from the ends of the earth saying, 'How false are the idols of our fathers, for there is no profit in them.'" And again he said: "I have placed you as a light among the gentiles that you might bring salvation to the end of the earth."

(39) And there I wish "to await the promise" of him who never deceives us. As he promises in the gospel: "They will come from the east and west to recline at the table of Abraham, Isaac, and Jacob." So we trust that believers will come from the whole earth.

(40) Thus it is proper for us to fish well and diligently, as the Lord warns and teaches us saying: "Follow me and I will make you fishermen of men." And again he says through the prophets: "Behold, I send forth fishermen and many hunters, says the Lord," and so forth. Thus we ought to cast our nets boldly to catch "a great multitude and crowd" for God, and to assure that there are clergy everywhere to baptize and preach to a people hungry and in need. As the Lord says in the gospel when he warns and teaches saying: "Go therefore now and teach all people baptizing them in the name of the Father and the Son and the Holy Spirit teaching them to observe all that I have taught you. And behold I am with you each day until the end of the age." And again he says: "Go therefore into the

usque ad consummationem saeculi;[bz] et iterum dicit: *Euntes ergo in mundum uniuersum praedicate euangelium omni creaturae; qui crediderit et baptizatus fuerit saluus erit; qui uero non crediderit condempnabitur;*[ca] et iterum: *Praedicabitur hoc euangelium regni in uniuerso mundo in testimonium omnibus gentibus et tunc ueniet finis;*[cb] et item Dominus per prophetam praenuntiat inquit: *Et erit in nouissimis diebus, dicit Dominus, effundam de spiritu meo super omnem carnem et prophetabunt filii uestri et filiae uestrae et iuuenes uestri uisiones uidebunt et seniores uestri somnia somniabunt et quidem super seruos meos et super ancillas meas in diebus illis effundam de spiritu meo et prophetabunt;*[cc] et *in Osee dicit: Vocabo non plebem meam plebem meam et non misericordiam consecutam misericordiam consecutam et erit in loco ubi dictum est: Non plebs mea uos, ibi uocabuntur filii Dei uiui.*[cd]

(41) Vnde autem Hiberione qui numquam notitiam Dei habuerunt nisi idola et inmunda usque nunc semper coluerunt quomodo nuper facta est plebs Domini et filii Dei nuncupantur, filii Scottorum et filiae regulorum monachi et uirgines Christi esse uidentur?

(42) Et etiam una benedicta Scotta genetiua nobilis pulcherrima adulta erat, quam ego baptizaui; et post paucos dies una causa uenit ad nos, insinuauit nobis responsum accepisse a nuntio Dei et monuit eam ut esset uirgo Christi et ipsa Deo proximaret: Deo gratias, sexta ab hac die optime et auidissime arripuit illud quod etiam omnes uirgines Dei ita hoc faciunt—non sponte patrum earum, sed et persecutiones patiuntur et improperia falsa a parentibus suis et nihilominus plus augetur numerus—et de genere nostro qui ibi nati sunt nescimus numerum eorum—praeter uiduas et continentes. Sed ex illis maxime laborant quae seruitio detinentur: usque ad terrores et minas assidue perferunt; sed

bz. Mt 28.19–20 ca. Mk 16.15 cb. Mt 24.14 cc. Acts 2.17–18 cd. Rom 9.25–26

whole world preaching the gospel to every creature. Whoever believes and is baptized will be saved, but whoever does not believe will be condemned." And again: "This gospel of the kingdom will be preached in the whole world as a testimony to all nations, and then the end will come." And again the Lord announced through the prophet saying: "There will be in the final days, says the Lord, a pouring forth of my spirit over all flesh, so that your sons and your daughters will prophesy, and your young men will see visions and your old men dream dreams. Indeed in those days I will pour out my spirit on my male and female servants and they will prophesy." And the prophet Hosea says: "I will call those not my people my people and her not beloved my beloved. And in the very place it was said to them that you are not my people, there they will be called the sons of the living God."

(41) How is it that those in Ireland who never had any knowledge of God—worshipping only idols and unclean things—have now become a people of the Lord and are called sons of God? The sons of the Irish and daughters of kings are indeed becoming monks and virgins of Christ.

(42) And indeed there was a blessed Irish woman of noble birth whom I had baptized who came to us after a few days for this very reason. She said she had received a divine call from a messenger of God to become a virgin of Christ and draw closer to God. Thanks be to God, six days later she laudably and avidly embraced this life that all virgins of God choose. The parents of these women do not approve and they suffer persecution and false accusations from them, but nevertheless their numbers continue to grow. We don't know how many have been born into the celibate life there from our efforts—not including widows and women who practice continence in marriage. But it is the slave women who suffer the most.[12] They are subjected to continuous harassment and terror. But the Lord

12. In early Irish society, a female slave (Old Irish *cumal*) was considered a basic unit of currency. Such slaves had no legal rights and could be treated however the master wished with impunity. See Kelly 1988, 95–97.

Dominus gratiam dedit multis ex ancillis suis, nam etsi uetantur tamen fortiter imitantur.

(43) Vnde autem etsi uoluero amittere illas et ut pergens in Brittanniis—et libentissime paratus eram quasi ad patriam et parentes; non id solum sed etiam usque ad Gallias uisitare fratres et ut uiderem faciem sanctorum Domini mei: scit Deus quod ego ualde optabam, sed alligatus Spiritu, qui mihi protestatur si hoc fecero, ut futurum reum me esse designat et timeo perdere laborem quem inchoaui, et non ego sed Christus Dominus, qui me imperauit ut uenirem esse cum illis residuum aetatis meae, si Dominus uoluerit et custodierit me ab omni uia mala, ut non peccem coram illo.

(44) Spero autem hoc debueram, sed memet ipsum non credo quamdiu fuero *in hoc corpore mortis*,[ce] quia fortis est qui cotidie nititur subuertere me a fide et praeposita castitate religionis non fictae usque in finem uitae meae Christo Domino meo, sed caro inimica semper trahit ad mortem, id est ad inlecebras inlicitate perficiendas; et scio ex parte quare uitam perfectam ego non egi sicut et ceteri credentes, sed confiteor Domino meo, et non erubesco in conspectu ipsius, *quia non mentior*,[cf] ex quo cognoui eum a iuuentute mea creuit in me amor Dei et timor ipsius, et usque nunc fauente Domino *fidem seruaui*.[cg]

(45) Rideat autem et insultet qui uoluerit, ego non silebo neque abscondo *signa et mirabilia*[ch] quae mihi a Domino monstrata sunt ante multos annos quam fierent, quasi qui nouit omnia etiam *ante tempora saecularia*.[ci]

(46) Vnde autem debueram sine cessatione Deo gratias agere, qui saepe indulsit insipientiae meae neglegentiae meae et de loco non in uno quoque ut non mihi uehementer irasceretur, qui adiutor datus sum et non cito adquieui secundum quod mihi ostensum fuerat et sicut *Spiritus suggerebat*,[cj] et *misertus est* mihi

ce. Rom 7.24. cf. Gal 1.20 cg. 2Tm 4.7 ch. Dn 6.27
ci. 2Tm 1.9 cj. Jn 14.26

gives grace to his many handmaids, for even though they are forbidden to follow him they imitate the Lord bravely.

(43) Thus even if I wished to leave these women and go to Britain—and I was quite prepared to visit my country and my family, and to go on to Gaul to see the face of the saints of my Lord—God knows I wanted that very much, but I am bound by the Spirit who declares that if I left I would be guilty of sin. I am afraid of abandoning the labor I have begun here—no, not I but Christ the Lord who ordered me to stay with these people for the rest of my life, if the Lord is willing, and will guard me from every evil path so that I may not sin in his presence.

(44) I hope, however, that I have done well, but I do not trust myself "as long as I am in this body of death," for strong is he who daily tries to turn me away from my faith and the true, pure chastity which I have chosen to the end of my life for Christ my Lord. But the hostile flesh always drags me towards death—that is, to those enticing, forbidden desires. I know that, in part, I have not led a perfect life like other believers. I confess this to my Lord and am not ashamed in his sight. "For I do not lie"—since I first came to know him as a young man the love of God and fear of him have grown in me, so that by the grace of the Lord "I have kept the faith" until now.

(45) Let whoever will laugh at and mock me, but I will not be silent nor will I hide the "signs and wonders" which were show to me by the Lord many years before they happened. For God knows everything "from before the world began."

(46) Therefore I should give thanks without ceasing to God who often forgave my foolishness and carelessness. On more than one occasion he did not show his anger against me who had been chosen as his helper—a helper slow to do what he revealed to me as "the Spirit reminded me." The Lord "was merciful to me a thousand

Dominus *in milia milium*,[ck] quia uidit in me quod paratus eram, sed quod mihi pro his nesciebam de statu meo quid facerem, quia multi hanc legationem prohibebant, etiam inter se ipsos pos tergum meum narrabant et dicebant: "Iste quare se mittit in periculo inter hostes qui Deum non nouerunt?"—non ut causa malitiae, sed non sapiebat illis, sicut et ego ipse testor, intellegi propter rusticitatem meam—et non cito agnoui gratiam quae tunc erat in me; nunc mihi sapit quod ante debueram.

(47) Nunc ergo simpliciter insinuaui fratribus et conseruis meis qui mihi crediderunt propter quod *praedixi et praedico*[cl] ad roborandam et confirmandam fidem uestram. Vtinam ut et uos imitemini maiora et potiora faciatis! Hoc erit gloria mea, quia *filius sapiens gloria patris est*.[cm]

(48) Vos scitis et Deus qualiter inter uos conuersatus sum a iuuentute mea in fide ueritatis et in sinceritate cordis. Etiam ad gentes illas inter quas habito, ego fidem illis praestaui et praestabo. Deus scit *neminem* illorum *circumueni*,[cn] nec cogito, propter Deum et ecclesiam ipsius, ne excitem illis et nobis omnibus persecutionem et ne per me blasphemaretur nomen Domini; quia scriptum est: *Vae homini per quem nomen Domini blasphematur*.[co]

(49) Nam *etsi imperitus sum in omnibus*[cp] tamen conatus sum quippiam seruare me etiam et fratribus Christianis et uirginibus Christi et mulieribus religiosis, quae mihi ultronea munuscula donabant et super altare iactabant ex ornamentis suis et iterum reddebam illis et aduersus me scandalizabantur cur hoc faciebam; sed ego propter spem perennitatis, ut me in omnibus caute propterea conseruarem, ita ut <non> me in aliquo titulo infideli caperent uel ministerium seruitutis meae nec etiam in minimo incredulis locum darem infamare siue detractare.

ck. Ex 20.6 cl. 2Cor 13.2 cm. Prv 10.1 cn. 2Cor 7.2
co. Rom 2.24; Mt 18.7 cp. 2Cor 11.6

thousand times" because he looked inside me and saw that I was ready, but did not know what to do in my confused state. There were many who tried to prevent my mission. They would talk behind my back and say: "Why does this man put himself in danger among barbarians who do not know God?" I can testify that they did not do this out of malice, but because they truly did not believe someone as admittedly rustic as myself could carry out such a task. I was not quick to acknowledge then the grace that was within me, as now I know I should have.

(47) Now I have given a simple account to my brothers and fellow servants who have believed me on account of what "I said and say still" in order to strengthen and confirm your faith. I wish that you would strive for greater things and perform greater deeds than I have accomplished! This will be my glory, for "a wise son is the glory of his father."

(48) You all know, as does God, how I have lived among you since my youth in true faith and sincerity of heart. Likewise among the heathen with whom I now live I have been faithful and will continue to be so. God knows that "I have taken advantage of no one." For the sake of God and his church I would never do so lest I provoke persecution of them and all of us, and lest because of me the name of the Lord be blasphemed. As it is written: "Woe to the one through whom the name of the Lord is blasphemed."

(49) For "although I am unskilled in all things," nevertheless I have tried somehow to preserve myself for the sake of my Christian brothers and the virgins of Christ and the religious women who of their own accord used to give me little gifts and lay some of their ornaments on the altar. I returned them and they were offended that I did this. But I did so in hope of lasting success, so that I might carefully preserve my work in the long term. I did not wish to give nonbelievers any chance to lay hold of me or criticize my ministry. Not even in the smallest matter would I give them the opportunity to speak against me or defame my character.

(50) Forte autem quando baptizaui tot milia hominum sperauerim ab aliquo illorum uel dimidio scriptulae? *Dicite mihi et reddam uobis.*[cq] Aut quando ordinauit ubique Dominus clericos per modicitatem meam et ministerium gratis distribui illis, si poposci ab aliquo illorum uel pretium uel calciamenti mei, *dicite aduersus me et reddam uobis.*[cr]

(51) Magis *ego impendi pro uobis*[cs] ut me caperent, et inter uos et ubique pergebam causa uestra in multis periculis etiam usque ad exteras partes, ubi nemo ultra erat et ubi numquam aliquis peruenerat qui baptizaret aut clericos ordinaret aut populum consummaret: donante Domino diligenter et libentissime pro salute uestra omnia generaui.

(52) Interim praemia dabam regibus praeter quod dabam mercedem filiis ipsorum qui mecum ambulant, et nihilominus comprehenderunt me cum comitibus meis et illa die auidissime cupiebant interficere me, sed tempus nondum uenerat, et omnia quaecumque nobiscum inuenerunt rapuerunt illud et me ipsum ferro uinxerunt, et quartodecimo die absoluit me Dominus de potestate eorum et quicquid nostrum fuit redditum est nobis propter Deum et *necessarios amicos*[ct] quos ante praeuidimus.

(53) Vos autem experti estis quantum ego erogaui illis qui iudicabant per omnes regiones quos ego frequentius uisitabam. Censeo enim non minimum quam pretium quindecim hominum distribui illis, ita ut me fruamini et ego uobis semper fruar in Deum. Non me paenitet nec satis est mihi: adhuc *impendo et superimpendam;*[cu] potens est Dominus ut det mihi postmodum ut meipsum *impendar pro animabus uestris.* [cv]

(54) Ecce *testem Deum inuoco in animam meam*[cw] *quia non mentior*[cx]: neque ut sit *occasio adulationis* uel *auaritiae*[cy] scripserim uobis neque ut honorem spero ab aliquo uestro; sufficit enim honor qui nondum uidetur sed corde creditur; *fidelis* autem *qui promisit:*[cz] *numquam mentitur.*[da]

cq. 1Sm 12.3
cr. 1Sm 12.3
cs. 2Cor 12.15
ct. Acts 10.24
cu. 2Cor 12.15
cv. 2Cor 12.15
cw. 2Cor 1.23
cx. Gal 1.20
cy. 1Thes 2.5
cz. Heb 10.23
da. Ti 1.2

(50) When I baptized so many thousands, did I perhaps expect even a trifle from them in return? "Tell me and I will repay you." Or when the Lord ordained clergy everywhere through my unworthiness and when I gave my ministry to them for free, if I asked from anyone even the price of my shoes, "testify against me and I will repay you."

(51) On the contrary, "I spent myself for you" so that they would receive me. I traveled among you everywhere risking many dangers for your sake even to the farthest places beyond which no one lived. No one had even gone that far to baptize or ordain clergy or serve the people. With God's help, I did all this carefully and most gladly for your salvation.

(52) Sometimes I did give presents to kings, in addition to the money I gave their sons who traveled with me. Even so, on one occasion they detained me with my friends and on that day very much desired to kill me. But my time had not yet come. They stole everything of value that we carried and put me in irons. But on the fourteenth day the Lord freed me from their power everything they had stolen from us was returned thanks to God and some "close friends" we had seen earlier.

(53) You all know how much I paid the judges in all those regions I frequently visited. I must have paid them the price of fifteen men so that you might enjoy me and I might enjoy you in God. I do not regret it nor do I intend to stop. "I spend and will spend more." The Lord is powerful so that that he may grant me that afterwards "I may spend myself for your souls."

(54) Behold, "I call God as my witness upon my soul" that I do not lie. Nor do I write this to you as "an occasion of flattery or greed." Nor do I write because I seek honor from any of you. The honor that is not yet seen but lies in the heart is enough for me. For "he who promised is faithful." "He never lies."

(55) Sed uideo iam *in praesenti saeculo*[db] me supra modum exaltatum a Domino, et non eram dignus neque talis ut hoc mihi praestaret, dum scio certissime quod mihi melius conuenit paupertas et calamitas quam diuitiae et diliciae. Sed et *Christus Dominus pauper* fuit *pro nobis*,[dc] ego uero miser et infelix etsi opes uoluero iam non habeo, *neque me ipsum iudico.*[dd] Quia cotidie spero aut internicionem aut circumueniri aut redigi in seruitutem siue occasio cuiuslibet; *sed nihil horum uereor*[de] propter promissa caelorum, quia iactaui meipsum in manus Dei omnipotentis, qui ubique dominatur, sicut propheta dicit: *Iacta cogitatum tuum in Deum et ipse te enutriet.*[df]

(56) Ecce nunc *commendo animam meam fidelissimo Deo*[dg] meo, *pro quo legationem fungor*[dh] in ignobilitate mea, sed quia *personam non accipit*[di] et elegit me ad hoc officium ut *unus* essem *de suis minimis*[dj] minister.

(57) Vnde autem *retribuam illi pro omnibus quae retribuit mihi.*[dk] Sed quid dicam uel quid promittam Domino meo, quia nihil ualeo nisi ipse mihi dederit? Sed *scrutator corda et renes*[dl] quia satis et nimis cupio et paratus eram ut donaret mihi *bibere calicem*[dm] eius, sicut indulsit et ceteris amantibus se.

(58) Quapropter non contingat mihi a Deo meo ut numquam amittam *plebem suam quam adquisiuit*[dn] in ultimis terrae. Oro Deum ut det mihi perseuerantiam et dignetur ut reddam illi testem fidelem usque ad transitum meum propter Deum meum.

(59) Et si aliquid boni umquam imitatus sum propter Deum meum, quem diligo, peto illi det mihi ut cum illis proselitis et captiuis pro nomine suo effundam sanguinem meum, etsi ipsam etiam caream sepulturam aut miserissime cadauer per singula membra diuidatur canibus aut bestiis asperis aut *uolucres caeli*

db. Gal 1.4
dc. 2Cor 8.9
dd. 1Cor 4.3
de. Acts 20.24
df. Ps 54.23
dg. Lk 23.46; 1Pt 4.19
dh. Eph 6.20
di. Dt 10.17; Gal 2.6
dj. Mt 25.40 ; cf. 1 Cor 15.9.
dk. Ps 115.12
dl. Ps 7.10
dm. Mt 20.23
dn. Is 43.21

(55) But I see now that "in this present age" I have been exalted highly by the Lord. I was not worthy of this nor the sort of person he should have honored so. I know very well that poverty and calamity are better suited to me than riches and pleasures. But "even as Christ was made poor for our sake," so I too am wretched and unfortunate. I have no wealth even if I wanted it, and "I am not judging myself." Every day I expect murder, kidnapping, a return to slavery, or whatever else may happen. "But I fear none of these things" because of the promises of heaven. I have cast myself into the hands of almighty God who rules everywhere. As the prophet says, "Cast your burden onto God and he will sustain you."

(56) Behold now "I commend my spirit to my most faithful God," "whose ambassador I am" in my unworthiness. But because God "does not play favorites" he chose me for this task that I might be "one of the least of his" servants.

(57) Therefore "I will give back to him for all that he has done for me." But what can I say or give to my Lord since all I have is a gift from him? But it is enough that "he searches the heart and the inmost parts" and knows that I was willing "to drink the cup" he had prepared for me, just as he gave it to the others who loved him.

(58) So may it never happen that my God would separate me from "the people he has purchased" in the ends of the earth. I pray to God that he give me perseverance and allow me to remain a faithful witness to him until the end of my life for the sake of my God.

(59) If I have ever imitated something good for the sake of my God whom I love, I ask him that I might be able to shed my blood with those proselytes and captives for his name's sake, even if this means I will lack a grave or that my poor body be torn apart by dogs or wild animals or "devoured by the birds of the air." I firmly believe

comederent illud.[do] Certissime reor, si mihi hoc incurrisset, lucratus sum animam cum corpore meo, quia sine ulla dubitatione in die illa resurgemus in claritate solis, hoc est in gloria Christi Iesu redemptoris nostri, quasi *filii Dei uiui*[dp] et *coheredes Christi*[dq] et *conformes futuri imaginis ipsius*;[dr] quoniam *ex ipso et per ipsum et in ipso*[ds] regnaturi sumus.

(60) Nam sol iste quem uidemus iubente propter nos cotidie oritur, sed numquam regnabit neque permanebit splendor eius, sed et omnes qui adorant eum in poenam miseri male deuenient; nos autem, qui credimus et adoramus solem uerum Christum, qui numquam interibit, neque *qui fecerit uoluntatem* ipsius, sed *manebit in aeternum quomodo et Christus manet in aeternum,*[dt] qui regnat cum Deo Patre omnipotente et cum Spiritu Sancto ante saecula et nunc et per omnia saecula saeculorum. Amen.

(61) Ecce iterum iterumque breuiter exponam uerba confessionis meae. *Testificor* in ueritate et in exultatione cordis *coram Deo et sanctis angelis eius*[du] quia numquam habui aliquam occasionem praeter euangelium et promissa illius ut umquam redirem ad gentem illam unde prius uix euaseram.

(62) Sed precor credentibus et timentibus Deum, quicumque dignatus fuerit inspicere uel recipere hanc scripturam quam Patricius peccator indoctus scilicet Hiberione conscripsit, ut nemo umquam dicat quod mea ignorantia, si aliquid pusillum egi uel demonstrauerim secundum Dei placitum, sed arbitramini et uerissime credatur quod donum Dei fuisset. Et haec est confessio mea antequam moriar.

do. Lk 8.5 dp. Rom 9.26 dq. Rom 8.17 dr. Rom 8.29
ds. Rom 11.36 dt. 1Jn 2.17; Jn 12.34 du. 1Tm 5.21

that if this should happen to me, I would have gained my soul as well as my body. For without any doubt on that day we shall rise again in the brightness of the sun which is the glory of Jesus Christ our redeemer. We will be "sons of the living God" and "fellow heirs with Christ" and "conformed to his image." For we shall reign "from him, through him, and in him."

(60) For the sun we see rises each day for us by God's command, but it will never reign nor will its splendor last. Moreover, those who worship it will come into wretched punishment. We, however, believe in and adore the true sun, Christ, who will never perish. Neither will anyone "who does the will" of him, but "will live forever just as Christ lives forever." Christ reigns with God the Father almighty and with the Holy Spirit since before time and now for all time to come. Amen.

(61) Behold, I have set forth the words of my declaration again and again. "I testify" in truth and from the joy of my heart "before God and his holy angels" that I have had no purpose in returning to the Irish, from who I once escaped, except to preach the gospel and the promises of God.

(62) I pray that any of you who believe in and fear God, whoever might come upon these words written in Ireland by Patrick the ignorant sinner, that you might judge and truly believe that any small thing I accomplished or did that was pleasing to God was done by the gift of God. This is my declaration before I die.

VITA SANCTI PATRICII

Prologus

Quoniam quidem, mi domine Aido, *multi conati sunt ordinare narrationem*[a] utique istam secundam quod patres eorum et qui ministri ab initio fuerunt sermonis tradiderunt illis, sed propter difficilimum narrationis opus diuersasque opiniones et plurimorum plurimas suspiciones numquam ad unum certumque historiae tramitem peruenierunt: ideo, ni fallor, iuxta hoc nostrorum prouerbium, ut deducuntur pueri in ambiteathrum in hoc periculossum et profundum narrationis sanctae pylagus turgentibus proterue gurgitum aggeribus inter acutissimos carubdes per ignota aequora insitos a nullis adhuc lintribus excepto tantum uno patris mei Coguitosi expertum atque occupatum ingenioli mei puerilem remi cymbam deduxi. Sed ne magnum de paruo uidear finguere, pauca haec de multis sancti Patricii gestis parua peritia, incertis auctoribus, memoria labili, attrito sensu, uili sermone, sed affectu pissimo caritatis sanctitatis tuae et auctoritatis imperio oboedens carptim grauatimque explicare aggrediar.

In nomine regis poli saluatoris huius chosmi.

Incipit prologus de uita sancti Patricii confessoris.

Tempus, locus et persona requiruntur. A passione autem dominu nostri Iesu Christi colliguntur anni .cccc.xxx.vi. usque ad

Prologue. This section is corrupt in the manuscripts. I omit an interpolation from a life of St. Basil included in Bieler's text (1979, 62–63).

a. Lk 1.1

MUIRCHÚ'S *LIFE OF ST. PATRICK*

Prologue

Indeed, my lord Áed,[1] "many have attempted to put in order an account" of this story following what they heard from their fathers and those who were storytellers from ancient times.[2] But because of the great difficulty in telling this tale, the conflicting opinions, and the numerous suspicions of many, they were never able arrive at the one, certain path of history. And so, if I may confess, just as in our proverb of boys being led forth into the arena, I set out into the dangerous and deep sea of sacred story-telling in my little boat amid rocky reefs and waves swelling high above me into an unknown waters, traveled by none before except my father Cogitosus.[3] But lest I seem to create something large out of something small, I shall only tell of a few of the many stories of holy Patrick. This I do using with little experience, drawing on uncertain authorities, with my poor memory and feeble intellect, and in an unpolished style. Still, I set forth obeying your command with the most pious affection of holy love on account of your charity and authority.

In the name of the king of heaven, the savior of the universe.

Here begins the prologue of the life of holy Patrick the confessor

Time, place, and person are required. From the passion of our Lord Jesus Christ one counts 436 years to the death of Patrick. I have

1. Áed, bishop of Sliébte from 661–688.

2. The prologue is deliberately rhetorical in style and modeled on the opening of the gospel of Luke (1.1–2).

3. Cogitosus was the author of the *Life of St. Brigit*, written earlier in the seventh century.

obitum Patricii. Inueni quattuor nomina in libro scripta Patricii abud Uldanum episcopum Concubrensum: Sanctus Magonus, qui est clarus; Sucsetus <***> ipse est Patricius, Cothirthiacus, quia seruiuit quattuor domibus magorum; et emit illum ab illis unus, cui nomen erat Milúch Mocuboin magus, et seruiuit illi septem annis. Patricius Calforni filius quattuor nomina habuit: Sochet quando natus est, Contice quando seruiuit, Mauonius quando legit, Patricius quando ordinatus est.

Liber Primus

(1) De ortu Patricii et eius prima captiuitate

(2) De nauigio eius cum gentibus et uexatione diserti, cibo sibi <et> gentilibus diuinitus delato

(3) De secunda captura, quam senis decies diebus ab inimicis pertulerat

(4) De susceptione sua a parentibus ubi agnouerunt eum

(5) De aetate eius quando iens uidere sedem apostolicam uoluit discere sapientiam

(6) De inuentione sancti Germani in Galliis, et ideo non exiuit ultra

(7) De aetate eius quando uissitauit eum anguelus, ut ueniret adhuc

(8) De reuersione eius de Gallis et ordinatione Palladii et mox morte eius

(9) De ordinatione eius ab Amathorege episcopo defuncto Palladio

(10) De rege gentili habeto in Temoria quando uenerat sanctus Patricius babtismum portans

discovered four names[4] of Patrick in a book of Ultán,[5] bishop of Connor: Holy Magonus, meaning "famous;" Socsetus ... Patrick's own name; Cothirthiacus, because he served four houses of druids. One of these named Míluch moccu Bóin[6] bought him and Patrick served in his house seven years. Patrick the son of Cualfarnius[7] thus had four names: Sochet when he was born, Cothirthiacus as a slave, Magonus while a student, and Patrick when he was ordained.

Book One

(1) The birth of Patrick and his first captivity
(2) His voyage with pagans and their anger in a deserted land, and how he obtained food from God for himself and them
(3) His second enslavement when he was held by enemies for sixty days
(4) His welcome by his parents when they recognized him
(5) His age when he set out for the apostolic see desiring to learn wisdom
(6) His meeting with holy Germanus in Gaul and thus he went no further
(7) His age when an angel visited him that he might return here
(8) His return from Gaul and the ordination of Palladius, who died soon thereafter
(9) His ordination by bishop Amathorex with Palladius dead
(10) The pagan king ruling at Tara when holy Patrick came bringing baptism

4. *Magonus* may be a British Celtic name ancestral to the later Welsh *Maun*. The name *Socsetus* (*Sochet* below in 1) may be derived from a Celtic god *Sucellos* known from both Gaul and Britain. *Cothirthiacus* is from Irish *cethir* ("four"), because of the story here that Patrick served four houses of druids (cf. Tírechán 1).

5. Ultán was bishop of Árdbraccan in Dál Conchubair (Connor) in Meath, died 657 (cf. Tírechán prologue).

6. Patrick does not name his master in his letters. Tírechán (1) says he was a druid.

7. *Calpornius* in Patrick (*Conf.* 1).

(11) De primo eius itenere in hac insola, ut se ipsum redemeret ó Miliucc priusquam alios a demonio traheret

(12) De morte Milcon et uerbo Patricii de semine eius

(13) De consilio sancti Patricii ubi hessitum est de celebratione primi pascae

(14) De oblatione primo pasca in hac insola facta

(15) De festiuitate gentili in Temoria eadem nocte qua sanctus Patricius pasca adorauit

(16) De gressu regis Loiguri de Temoria ad Patricium in nocte Pascae

(17) De uocatione Patricii ad regem et fide Eirc filii Dego <et> morte magi in illa nocte

(18) De ira regis et suorum ad Patricium et plaga Dei super eos et transfinctione Patricii coram gentilibus

(19) De aduentu Patricii in die pascae ad Temoriam et fide Dubthaich maccu Lugir

(20) De conflictu Patricii aduersus magnum in illa <die> et mirabilibus uirtutibus

(21) De conuersione Loiguri regis et de uerbo Patricii de regno eius post se

(22) De doctrina et babtismate signisque sancti Patricii secundum exemplum Christi

(23) De morte Moneisen Saxonissae

(24) De conflictu sancti Patricii aduersum Coirthech regem Aloo

(25) De eo quod sanctus Patricius uidit caelum apertum et filium Dei et angelos eius

(26) De Macc Cuill et conuersione eius ad uerbum Patricii

(27) De gentibus laborantibus die dominica trans praeceptum Patricii

(28) De fabula Dairi et equo et oblatione Airdd Machae ad Patricium

(29) De fructifera terra in salsuginem uersa ad uerbum Patricii

Haec pauca de sancti Patricii peritia et uirtutibus Muirchu maccu Machtheni dictante Aiduo Slebtiensis ciuitatis episcopo conscripsit.

(11) His first journey on this island to buy his freedom from Miliucc before rescuing others from the devil
(12) The death of Miliucc and what Patrick said about his offspring
(13) The plan of holy Patrick when the celebration of the first Easter was discussed
(14) When Easter was first celebrated on this island
(15) The pagan festival held at Tara on the same night holy Patrick celebrated Easter
(16) How King Loíguire went out to meet Patrick on Easter night
(17) The summoning of Patrick to the king and how Erc son of Daig believed and the death of a druid that night
(18) The anger of the king and his followers against Patrick, and the plague of God against them, and Patrick's transformation before the eyes of the pagans
(19) Patrick's arrival at Tara on Easter and the faith of Dubthach moccu Lugir
(20) The contest of Patrick and the druid on that day and his miraculous deeds
(21) The conversion of King Loíguire and the word of Patrick concerning his kingdom after him.
(22) The teaching, baptism, and miracles of holy Patrick following the example of Christ
(23) The death of Moneisen the Saxon
(24) The conflict of holy Patrick with Coirthech, king of Ail
(25) How holy Patrick saw the heavens open and beheld the Son of God and his angels
(26) Mac Cuill and his conversion at the word of Patrick
(27) The pagans working on Sunday against the teaching of Patrick
(28) The story of Dáire and his horse, and his offering of Armagh to Patrick
(29) How the word of Patrick turned a swamp into fertile land

These few words concerning the tradition of holy Patrick and his miraculous deeds are recorded by Muirchú moccu Machtheni at the request of Aéd bishop of Sléibte.

De natali S. Patricii et de eius captiuitate in Hibernia

(1.1) Patricius, qui et Sochet uocabatur, Brito natione in Britannis natus, Cualfarnio diacono ortus, filio, ut ipse ait, Potiti presbiteri, qui fuit uico Bannauem Thaburniae, chaut procul a mari nostro, quem uicum constanter indubitanterque conperimus esse Ventre, matre etiam conceptus Concessa nomine, annorum sedecim puer cum ceteris captus in hanc barbarorum insulam aduectus est <et> apud quendam gentilem immitemque regem ii seruitute detentus. Qui sexennem more Hebraico *cum timore* Dei *et tremore*[b] secundum psalmiste sententiam in uigiliis et orationibus multis—cencies in die et cencies in nocte orabat—libenter *reddiens quae Dei sunt Deo et quae Caesaris Caesari*[c] incipiensque timere Deum et amare omnipotentem Dominum; nam usque ad id temporis ignorabat Deum uerum, sed tunc spiritus feruebat in eo. Post multas ibi tribulationes, post famem et sitim, post frigora et nuditates, post pascenda pecora, post frequentias angelici Victorici a Deo ad illum missi, post magnas uirtutes omnibus pene notas, post responsa diuina, e quibus unum aut duo haec exempli tantum gracia demonstrabo: "Bene ieiunas, cito iturus ad patriam tuam," et iterum: "Ecce nauis tua parata est," quae non erat prope sed forte habebat ducenta milia passuum, ubi numquam habuerat iter; post haec omnia, ut diximus, quae enumerari poene a nemine possunt, cum ignotis barbaris gentilibusque hominibus

b. Ps 54.6; Eph 6.5 c. Mt 22.21

The Birth of St. Patrick and His Captivity in Ireland

(1.1) Patrick, who was called Sochet, was a Briton by birth and born in Britain. His father was Cualfarnius, a deacon, the son, as Patrick tells us, of the priest Potitus, who lived in Bannavem Thaburniae,[8] not far from our sea. This place, as I am reliably and beyond doubt informed, is what is now called Ventre. His mother's name was Concessa.[9] When he was a boy of sixteen, he was taken with others to this barbarian island and held in slavery by a cruel pagan king. He served him for six years according to Hebrew law[10] "with fear" of God "and trembling," as the Psalmist says, with vigils and many prayers—he prayed a hundred times by day and a hundred by night—gladly "giving to God what were the things of God and to Caesar the things of Caesar." He began to fear and love the almighty Lord. For until that time he was ignorant of the true God, but now his spirit began to burn within him. After many hardships, after hunger and thirst, after cold and nakedness, after tending sheep, after frequent visits from Victoricus, an angel sent by God,[11] after many well-known miracles, after divine messages—I will mention only two examples: "You have fasted well,[12] soon you will return to your country," and "Behold your ship is ready," which was not nearby but perhaps two hundred miles away where he had never been—after all these things which hardly anyone could recount, at the age of twenty-three he left his pagan master to his own actions

8. Patrick's *Bannaventa Berniae* (*Conf.* 1), which Muirchú places near the Irish Sea at an unknown town named *Ventre*—perhaps *Venta Silurum* in south-east Wales, in the county now known as *Gwent*.

9. Patrick does not give his mother's name. At Corbridge in northeast England near Hadrian's Wall, a Roman altar was found with a dedication by a prefect of cavalry named *Quintus Calpurnius Concessinius*, with forms of the names of both Patrick's father and mother. If Muirchú's information is accurate, this Roman officer may have been an ancestor of Patrick (Collingwood and Wright 1965, vol.1 #1142).

10. V. Ex 21.2, Dt 15.12. A Hebrew slave was to serve six years and be freed in the seventh.

11. An angel here, but according to Patrick (*Conf.* 23) a human voice in his dream.

12. Cf. Conf. 17.

multos et falsos deos adorantibus iam in naui sibi parata deserto tiranno gentilique homine cum actibus suis et accepto caelesti eternoque Deo in comitatu sancto ex praecepto diuino aetatis uigesimo tertio ad Britanias nauigauit.

(1.2) Ternis itaque diebus totidemque noctibus quasi ad modum Ionae in mari cum iniquis fluctuans, postea bis denis simul et octenis diurnis luminibus Moysico more alio licet sensu per desertum fatigatus, murmurantibus gentilibus quasi Iudei fame et siti pene deficientibus conpulsus, a gubernatore temptatus atque ut illis deum suum ne perirent oraret rogatus, mortalibus exoratus, turbae misertus, spiritu contribulatus, merito coronatus, a Deo magnificatus, abundantiam cibi ex grege porcorum a Deo misso sibi uelut ex coturnicum turma Deo aiuuate praebuit. Mel quoque siluestre et quondam Iohanni subuenit, motatis tamen pessimorum gentilium merito porcinis carnibus pro locustarum usu. Ille autem nichil gustans de his cibis—immolaticium enim erat—nec esuriens nec sitiens mansit illesus. Eadem uero nocte dormiens temptauit satanas grauiter, fingens saxa ingentia et quasi comminuentia membra; sed inuocato Helia bina uoce ortus est ei sol, qui refulgens expulit omnes caliginum tenebras, et restitutae sunt ei uires eius.

(1.3) Et iterum post multos annos capturam ab alienigenis pertulit, ubi prima nocte audire meruit responsum diuinum sibi dicens: "Duobus mensibus eris cum illis, id est cum inimicis tuis." Quod ita factum est: sexagesimo enim die liberauit eum Dominus de manibus eorum, praeuidens ei cum comitibus suis cibum et ignem et siccitatem quottidie donec decimo die peruenerunt ad homines.

(1.4) Et iterum post paucos annos ut antea in patria sua propria apud parentes suos requieuit, qui ut filium susceperunt rogantes illum ut uel sic post tantas tribulationes et temptationes de reliquo uitae numquam ab illis discederet. Sed ille non consensit, et ibi ostensae sunt ei multae uisiones.

and with the sacred companionship of eternal God sailed in the ship prepared for him to Britain with pagan barbarians who worshipped many false gods.

(1.2) After three days and nights at sea, like Jonah, with these wicked men, he afterwards was marched twenty-eight days through a desert, like Moses, though in a slightly different way. The pagans grumbled, like the Jews, that they were nearly dead from hunger and thirst. Their captain taunted him, asking him to call on his god to save them from death. Moved by their suffering, having pity on the men, suffering in his spirit, crowned with merit, and glorified by God, Patrick supplied them with plentiful food, with God's help, from a herd of pigs, just as God had sent a flock of quails to the Jews. They also found wild honey, like John the Baptist, but as was fitting for wicked pagans they received pigs instead of locusts. Patrick, however, ate none of it—it had been offered in sacrifice—but he remained well suffering neither hunger or thirst. On that same night while he was sleeping, Satan attacked him violently. Patrick felt as if he was under great rocks crushing his limbs. But he called on Elijah twice and the sun rose on him, scattering all the shadows of darkness and restoring his strength.

(1.3) And again after many years he was again captured by strangers. On the first night he was granted a divine message that said to him: "You will be with them for two months,[13] that is, with your enemies." And thus it was. After sixty days the Lord freed him from their hands, providing Patrick and his companions with food, fire, and water every day until on the tenth day they found other people.

(1.4) And again after a few years Patrick was, as in his youth, back in his own country with his parents, who welcomed him home as a son begging him that after so many tribulations and difficulties he would never leave them again. But he did not agree, and there received many visions.

13. Cf. Conf. 21.

(1.5) Et erat annorum triginta secundum apostolum *in uirum perfectum in mensuram aetatis plenitudinis Christi.*[d] Egressus ad sedem apostolicam uisitandam et honorandam, ad caput utique omnium ecclesiarum totius mundi, ut sapientiam diuinam sanctaque misteria ad quae uocauit illum Deus ut disceret atque intellegeret et inpleret, et ut praedicaret et donaret diuinam graciam in nationibus externis conuertens ad fidem Christi.

(1.6) Transnauigato igitur mari dextro Britannico ac cepto itinere per Gallias, Alpes ad extremum, ut corde proposuerat, transcensurus quendam sanctisimum episcopum Altsiodori ciuitate principem Germanum summum donum inuenit, aput quem non paruo tempore demoratus, iuxta id quod Paulus ad pedes Gamaliel fuerat, in omni subiectione et patientia atque oboedientia scientiam sapientiam castitatemque et omnem utilitatem tam spiritus quam animae cum magno Dei timore et amore in bonitate et simplicitate cordis, corpore et spiritu uirgo, toto animi desiderio didicit dilexit custodiuit.

(1.7) Peractisque ibi multis temporibus quasi ut alii quadraginta alii triginta annis ille antiquus ualde fidelis Victoricus nomine, qui omnia sibi in Hibernica seruitute possito antequam essent dixerat, eum crebris uissionibus uissitauit dicens ei adesse tempus ut ueniret et aeuanguelico rete nationes feras et barbaras ad quas docendas misserat illum Deus ut piscaret, ibique ei dictum est in uissione: "Vocant te filii et filiae siluae Foclitae" et caetera.

(1.8) Opportuno ergo tempore imperante comitante diuino auxilio coeptum ingreditur iter ad opus in quod ollim praeparatus fuerat, utique aeuanguelii, et missit Germanus seniorem cum illo, hoc est Segitium praespiterum, ut testem comitem haberet, quia nec adhuc a sancto domino Germano in pontificali gradu

d. Eph 4.13

(1.5) Now he was thirty years old and, as the apostle says, "a mature man in the measure of the fullness of Christ." He left to visit and honor the apostolic see, the head of all the churches of the whole world. He desired to learn and understand and be filled with the divine wisdom and holy mysteries to which God was calling him, that he might preach and bring divine grace to distant people converting them to faith in Christ.

(1.6) Crossing the sea south of Britain and beginning his journey across Gaul, Patrick hoped to cross the Alps to his final destination. On the way he discovered the wonderful gift of a very holy bishop of the city of Auxerre, the great Germanus.[14] Patrick stayed with him a long time, just as Paul sat at the feet of Gamaliel. There with all discipline, patience, and obedience he learned knowledge, wisdom, chastity, and everything useful for mind and soul. With great fear of God, with love of goodness, simplicity of heart, a virgin in body and spirit, he learned, loved, and practiced the joy of his heart.

(1.7) After spending a long time in Gaul—some say forty years, others thirty—his old and faithful friend Victoricus, who had told him everything that would happen while he was a slave in Ireland, came to him in frequent visions saying the time had now come to fish with the net of the Gospel among the wild barbarians to whom God had sent him to teach. He was told in a vision: "The sons and daughters of the wood of Foclut[15] call you," etc.

(1.8) So when the right moment came Patrick set out with divine help on that journey of the Gospel for which he had long been prepared. Germanus sent with him the priest Segitus that he might have a fellow witness, because Patrick had not yet been ordained a bishop by the holy lord Germanus. They knew that Palladius,[16] archdeacon

14. Germanus (*c.* 375-*c.* 437) Bishop of Auxerre from 418, he travelled to Britain in 429 and 436 to battle the Pelagian heresy popular there. Patrick never mentions him in his letters.

15. Cf. Conf. 23, Tírechán 14.

16. Palladius was sent by Pope Celestine "to the Irish believers as their first bishop" according to the chronicle of Prosper under the year 431 (Mommsen I.473).

ordinatus est. Certi enim erant quod Paladius archdiaconus pape Caelestini urbis Romae episcopi, qui tunc tenebat sedem apostolicam quadragensimus quintus a sancto Petro apostolo, ille ordinatus et missus fuerat ad hanc insolam sub brumali rigore possitam conuertendam. Sed prohibuit illum quia *nemo potest accipere quicquam de terra nissi datum ei fuerit de caelo.*[e] Nam neque hii fieri et inmites homines facile reciperunt doctrinam eius neque et ipse longum uoluit transegere tempus in terra non sua, sed reuersus ad eum qui missit illum. Reuertente uero eo hinc et primo mari transito coeptoque terrarum itenere in Britonum finibus uita functus.

(1.9) Audita itaque morte sancti Paladii in Britannis, quia discipuli Paladii, id est Augustinus et Benedictus et caeteri, redeuntes retulerant in Ebmoria de morte eius, Patricius et qui cum eo erant declinauerunt iter ad quendam mirabilem hominem summum aepiscopum Amathorege nomine in propinquo loco habitantem, ibique sanctus Patricius *sciens quae euentura essent*[f] sibi episcopalem gradum ab Amathorege sancto episcopo accepit; etiam Auxilius Isarninusque et caeteri inferioris gradus eodem die quo sanctus Patricius ordinatus est. Tum acceptis benedictionibus perfectis omnibus secundum morem, cantato etiam Patricio quasi specialiter et conuenienter hoc psalmistae uorsu: *Tu es sacerdos in aeternum secundum ordinem Melchisedech*,[g] uenerabilis uiator paratam nauim in nomine sanctae Trinitatis ascendit et peruenit Brittannias et omissis omnibus ambulandi anfractibus praeter commone uiae officium—nemo enim dissidia quaerit Dominum—cum omni uelocitate flatuque prospero mare nostrum contendit.

(1.10) In illis autem diebus quibus haec gesta sunt in praedictis regionibus fuit rex quidam magnus ferox gentilisque, imperator barbarorum regnans in Temoria, quae erat caput Scotorum, Loiguire nomine filius Neill, origo stirpis regiae huius pene insolae.

e. Jn 3.27 f. Jn 18.4 g. Ps 109.4

of Pope Celestine, bishop of the city of Rome and forty-fifth in succession from St. Peter the apostle, had been ordained and sent to convert this island in the cold north. But he was prevented because "no one is able to receive anything unless it has been given by heaven." These wild and hostile people would not accept his teachings and he did wish to spend much time in a land not his own, so he returned to the one who had sent him. But on his way back from here, having crossed the first sea and started his journey, he died in the land of the Britons.

(1.9) At Ebmoria Patrick heard of the death of holy Palladius in Britain from his returning disciples Augustine, Benedict, and others. They then detoured to meet a certain remarkable man and great bishop named Amathorex who lived nearby. There holy Patrick, "knowing what would happen" to him, accepted the rank of bishop from the holy bishop Amathorex. Auxilius, Iserninus, and the rest received lesser grades on the same day Patrick was ordained. While they were accepting the blessings according to custom, they sang the words of the Psalmist as if especially and appropriately for Patrick: "You are a priest in the eternal order of Melchizedek." The experienced traveler then went on board a waiting ship and in the name of the holy Trinity crossed to Britain. Permitting no delays not required by the ordinary conditions of such a journey—for no one seeks the Lord with idleness—he crossed our sea quickly with a favorable wind.

(1.10) In those days in which these things happened there was in those regions a certain pagan king, mighty and fierce, the ruler of the barbarians ruling in Tara,[17] the capital of the Irish. His name was Loíguire son of Níall, whose family ruled almost all of

17. The hill of Tara, in County Meath, was the traditional seat of the high kings of Ireland.

Hic autem sciuos et magos et aurispices et incantatores et omnis malae artis inuentores habuerat, qui poterant omnia scire et prouidere ex more gentilitatis et idolatriae antequam essent; e quibus duo prae caeteris praeferebantur, quorum nomina haec sunt: Lothroch qui et Lochru, et Lucetmael qui et Ronal, et hii duo ex sua arte magica crebrius profetabant morem quendam exterum futurum in modum regni cum ignota quadam doctrina molesta longinquo trans maria aduectum, a paucis dictatum, a multis susceptum, ab omnibus honorandam, regna subuersurum, resistentes reges occissurum, turbas seducturum, omnes eorum deos distructurum, et iectis omnibus illorum artis operibus in saecula regnaturum. Portantem quoque suadentemque hunc morem signauerunt et profetauerant hiis uerbis quasi in modum ueriiculi crebo ab hiisdem dictis, maxime in antecedentibus aduentum Patricii duobus aut tribus annis. Haec autem sunt uersiculi uerba, propter linguae idioma non tam manifesta:

Adueniet ascicaput cum suo ligno curuicapite,
ex sua domu capite perforata incantabit nefas
a sua mensa ex anteriore parte domus suae,
respondebit ei sua familia tota "fiat, fiat."

Quod nostris uerbis potest manifestius expraemi: "Quando ergo haec omnia fiant, regnum nostrum, quod est gentile, non stabit." Quod sic postea euenerat; euersis enim in aduentu Patricii idulorum culturis fides Christi catholica nostra repleuit omnia. De his ista sufficiant; redeamus ad propossitum.

(1.11) Consummato igitur nauigio sancto perfectoque honerata nauis sancti cum transmarinis mirabilibus spiritalibusque tessauris quasi in opportunum portum in regiones Coolennorum,

this island. He surrounded himself with wise men, druids, soothsayers, sorcerers, and every sort skilled in the evil arts. They were able to know and foresee every event before it happened. Two of these the king preferred above all the rest—Lothroch, also called Lochru, and Lucet Máel, known as Ronal. These two by their magical arts frequently foretold of a foreign way of life about to arrive, a kind of kingdom from far across the sea bringing unknown and troublesome doctrines. Only a few would come teaching this doctrine, but it would be received by many. It would be honored by all and overthrow kingdoms. Rulers who resisted it would be slain, the crowds would be seduced, all their gods would be destroyed, their skills and works would be banished, and the new teaching would reign forever. They told of the man who would bring this new teaching and persuade the people. They prophesied about him in the following words in a kind of poem that was often recited, especially in the two or three years before Patrick's arrival. These are the words of the poem, though because of the strange language it is not very clear:

> There will arrive a shaven-head man with a stick bent in the head.
> He will chant evils songs from his house with a hole in its head.
> From his table at the front of his house,
> his family will reply to him: "Let it be, let it be."

In our own language[18] we can say this more clearly: "When these things come to pass, our pagan kingdom will not stand." This is of course what happened afterwards, when Patrick came and destroyed the worship of idols and the universal faith of Christ filled our land. But enough of these things—let us return to our story.

(1.11) Thus with his holy journey at an end, the boat of the holy man, heavy with marvels and spiritual treasures from across the sea, reached a suitable harbor in the region of Cúala,[19] a well-known

18. Muirchú was a native speaker of Irish.

19. Cúala robably at the mouth of the Avoca River in County Wicklow. Many of the places recorded in Muirchú's *Life* are unknown or their location is open to debate.

in portum apud nos clarum qui uocatur hostium Dee dilata est; ubi uissum est ei nihil perfectius esse quam ut semet ipsum primitus redemeret; et inde appetens sinistrales fines ad illum hominem gentilem Milcoin, apud quem quondam in captiuitate fuerat, portansque ei geminum seruitutis praetium, terrenum utique et caeleste, ut de capiuitate liberaret illum cui ante captiuus seruierat, ad anteriorem insolam, quae eius nomine usque hodie nominatur, prurim nauis conuertit. Tum deinde Brega Conalneosque fines nec non et fines Ulathorum in leuo dimittens ad extremum in quoddam fretum quod est Brene se inmissit. Et discenderunt in terram ad hostium Slain ille et qui cum eo erant in naui et absconderunt nauiculam et uenierunt aliquantulum in regionem ut requiescerent ibi, et inuenit eos porcinarius cuiusdam uiri natura boni licet gentilis, cui nomine erat Dichu, habitans ibi ubi nunc est orreum Patricii nomine cognominatum. Porcinarius autem putans eos fures aut latrones exiuit et indicauit domino suo du Dichoin et induxit illum super eos ignorantibus illis. Qui corde propossuerat occidere eos, sed uidens faciem sancti Patricii conuertit Dominus ad bonum cogitationes eius, et praedicauit Patricius fidem illi et ibi credidit Patricio prae omnibus et requiescit ibi sanctus apud illum non multis diebus. Sed uolens cito ire ut uissitaret praedictum hominem Milcoin et portaret ei praetium suum et uel sic conuerteret ad Christi fidem, relicta ibi nauis apud Dichoin coepit per terras diregere uiam in regiones Cruidnenorum donec peruenit ad montem Miss, de quo monte multo ante tempore quo ibi captiuus seruierat praeso uestigio in petra alterius montis expedito gradu uidit anguelum Victoricum in conspectu eius ascendisse in caelum.

(1.12) Audiens autem Miliucc seruum suum iturum ad uissitandum eum, ut morem quem nolebat in fine uitae faceret quasi per uim, ne seruo subiectus fieret et ille sibi dominaret instinctu

port of ours named Inber Dee. There nothing seemed more fitting to him than to redeem himself from slavery. He was therefore eager to journey north to the man Miliucc who had held him in captivity, bearing with him twice the ransom, both earthly and heavenly, that he might redeem from slavery the man who had once held him captive. He turned his boat towards the island today named for him,[20] then leaving Brega and the lands of Conaille and the Ulaid on one side, he sailed to the inlet of Bréne. There he and those with him landed the boat at Inber Slane and his their boat, going a little ways inland to rest. A swineherd found them there, a servant of a man of natural goodness named Díchu, who lived in the barn now named after Patrick. The swineherd thinking they were thieves and robbers ran to tell his master Díchu and quietly led him to them. Díchu had planned to kill them, but when he saw the face of holy Patrick, God changed his mind to good. Patrick preached the faith to him and Díchu believed, the first man to do so, and thus Patrick stayed with him several days. But Patrick was anxious to find Miluicc and buy his freedom[21] as well as convert him to faith in Christ, so he left his boat with Díchu and set out across the lands of the Cruithni until he reached Slíab Miss.[22] This was the mountain where he had been held captive many years before and had seen the angel Victoricus leave his footprint as he swiftly ascended into heaven.

(1.12) When Miliucc heard that his slave was on his way to see him, he decided he did not want to change his ways as if by force at the end of his life. So that the man he had enslaved might not

20. This island was probably one of the Skerries, County Dublin (cf. Tírechán 3). In this journey by boat, Patrick is sailing north along the coast from County Wicklow to County Down.

21. According to Irish law, Patrick was still a runaway slave.

22. *Slíab Miss*: Slemish, County Antrim.

diabuli sponte se igni tradidit et in domu in qua prius habitauerat rex congregato ad se omni instrumento substantiae suae incensus est. Stans autem sanctus Patricius in praedicto loco a latere dextero montis Miss, ubi primum illam regionem in qua seruiuit cum tali gratia adueniens uidit, ubi nunc usque crux habetur in signum ad uissum primum illius regionis, illico sub oculis rogum regis incensum intuitus. Stupefactus igitur ad hoc opus duabus aut tribus fere horis nullum uerbum proferens, suspirans et gemens lacrimansque atque haec uerba promens ait: "Nescio Deus scit, hic homo rex, qui se ipsum igni tradidit ne crederet in fine uitae suae et ne seruiret Deo aeterno, nescio Deus scit, nemo de filiis eius sedebit rex super sedem regni eius a generatione in generationem. Insuper et semen eius seruiet in sempiternum." Et his dictis orans et armans se signo crucis conuertit cito iter suum ad regiones Ulothorum per eadem uestigia quibus uenerat et rursum peruenit in campum Inis ad Dichoin ibique mansit diebus multis et circumiit totum campum et elegit et amauit et coepit fides crescere ibi.

(2.15) Ad promissa iterum recurrat oratio. Anguelus ad eum in omni septima die septimanae semper uenire consuerat et sicut homo cum homine loquitur ita conloquio angueli fruebatur Patricius. Etiam in sexto decimo anno aetatis captus et sex annis seruiuit et per triginta uices conductionum anguelus ad eum uenerat et consiliis atque conloquiis fruebatur anguelicis antequam de Scotia ad Latinos pergeret. Aliquando sues custodiens perdidit eas et anguelus ueniens ad eum sues indicauit illi. Aliquando etiam anguelus illi loquens multa illi dixit et postquam illi locutus est pedem supra petram ponens in Scirit in montem Mis coram se ascendit et uestigia pedis angueli in petra hucusque manentia cernuntur. Et in loco triginta uicibus ad eum locutus est; et ille locus orandi locus est et ibi fidelium praeces fructum felicissimum obtinent.

2.15 This passage is out of sequence in the text, though it is unclear exactly where it belongs. It is plainly a separate chapter, though it lacks a heading in the manuscripts. I follow Bieler's edition in placing it here.

rule over him, Miliucc, prompted by the devil, decided to destroy himself by fire. He brought together all his goods into the house where he had ruled as king and set fire to it and himself. Holy Patrick was standing on the right-hand side of Slíab Miss where now he had his first view of the region of his enslavement and grace since his return. There he saw the fire of Miliucc with his own eyes. Patrick was so stunned by the sight that he stood there for two or three hours without speaking, sighing and moaning and weeping. Then he spoke: "I do not know, God knows. This man at the end of his life gives himself over to fire rather than serve the eternal God. I do not know, God knows. None of his sons will rule over his kingdom from generation to generation. His descendants shall be subject to others forevermore." When he had said this he prayed and armed himself with the sign of the cross, then he turned and went back to the lands of the Ulaid along the same way he had come. He returned to Mag Inis and Díchu, remaining there several days traveling around the whole plain. He choose the area as a place he loved and there the faith began to grow.

(2.15) Let us return again to the material above. An angel used to come to him on the seventh day of every week. As one man speaks with another, so Patrick enjoyed conversing with the angel. Even when he was captured at the age of sixteen and endured six years of slavery, the angel came and spoke with him thirty times. Patrick enjoyed his conversations and counsels before he traveled from Ireland to the land of the Latins. Once while he was watching over pigs he lost them, and the angel came and showed him where they were. On another day after they had been speaking about many things, the angel placed his foot on the rock of Scirit next to Slíab Mís and rose in his presence. The footprint can still be seen. That is the place where the angel spoke to him thirty times. It is now a place of prayer where the prayers of the faithful yield happy fruit.

(1.13) Adpropinquauit autem pasca in diebus illis, quod pasca primum Deo in nostra Aegipto huius insolae uelut quondam in Gessen celebratum est, in inuenierunt consilium, ubi hoc primum pasca in gentibus ad quas missit illum Deus celebrarent, multisque super hac re consiliis iectis postremo inspirato diuinitus sancto Patricio uissum est hanc magnam Domini sollempnitatem quasi caput omnium sollempnitatem in campo Breg maximo, ubi erat regnum maximum nationum harum, quod erat caput omnis gentilitatis et idolatriae, liberari, ut iuxta uocem psalmistae *caput draconis confringeret*[h] et uti hic inuictus cuneus in caput totius idolatriae, ne possit ulterius aduersus Christi fidem insurgere, sub malleo fortis operis cum fide iuncti sancti Patricii et suorum manibus spiritalibus primus inlideretur. Et sic factum est.

(1.14) Eleuata igitur nauis ad mare et dimisso in fide plena et pace bono illo uiro Dichu migrantes de campo Iniss dexteraque manu demittentes omnia ad plenitudinem ministerii quae erant ante non incongrue leua in portum hostii Colpdi bene et prospere delati sunt, relictaque ibi naui pedistri itenere uenierunt in praedictum maximum campum, donec postremo ad uesperum peruenierunt ad ferti uirorum Feec, quam, ut fabulae ferunt, foderunt uiri, id est serui Feec ol Ferchertni qui fuerat unus e nouim magis profetis Bregg, fixoque ibi tentorio debeta pascae uota *sacrificiumque laudis*[i] cum omni deuotione spiritus Patricius cum suis Deo altissimo secundum profetae uocem reddidit.

(1.15) Contigit uero in illo anno ut aliam idolatriae sollempnitatem, quam gentiles incantationibus multis et magicis inuentionibus nonnullisque aliis idolatriae superstitionibus, congregatis etiam regibus, satrapis, ducibus, principibus et optimatibus populi, insuper et magis, incantatoribus, auruspicibus et omnis artis omnisque doni inuentoribus doctoribus uocatis ad Loigaireum uelut quondam ad Nabucodonossor regem in Temoria istorum Babylone exercere consuerant, eadem nocte qua sanctus

h. Ps 73.14 i. Tb 8.19; Cf. Heb. 13.15.

(1.13) In those days Easter was approaching. This was the first Easter celebrated in the Egypt of this island as in the Land of Goshen. They took counsel as to where they might celebrate this first Easter among the gentiles to which God had sent them. After discussing many possibilities, at last holy Patrick was inspired by God decided that this great solemn festival of the Lord, the greatest of all festivals, should be celebrated in the great plain of Brega. There was the greatest kingdom of all the tribes, the head of all their paganism and idolatry. There he would, as the Psalmist says, "crush the head of the dragon" and drive a wedge into the head of all idolatry that no other faith might rise against Christ. This would be done for the first time with the hammer of brave deeds joined to faith by the spiritual hands of holy Patrick and his companions. And thus it was done.

(1.14) They set out to sea in their ship from Mag Inis and left behind that good man Díchu full of peace and faith. In the fullness of their ministry they sailed with the coast on their right hand, as is proper, since it was on their left side before. After a good and calm trip they arrived at Inber Colpdi,[23] leaving behind their boat and traveling by foot to that great plain. As evening fell they at last arrived at the burial mounds of the men of Fíacc—Ferchertne, one of the nine wise prophets of Brega, says that it was built by the men, that is the servants, of Fíacc. There Patrick and his companions made camp and offered the proper Easter "sacrifice of praise" to the most high God with all devotion of spirit, just as the prophet says.

(1.15) At that same time another ceremony was being held which the pagans celebrated with many incantations, magical rites, and idolatrous superstitions. There were also kings, satraps, leaders, princes, and all the nobility, along with wizards, fortunetellers, and all those skilled in the dark arts summoned to Tara by Loíguire just as King Nebuchadnezzar had once called like men to Babylon.[24] They held their pagan festival on the same night that Patrick was celebrating Easter. There was also a law among them announced to

23. Inber Colpdi was at the mouth of the River Boyne.
24. V. Dn 3.2–3.

Patricius pasca illi illam adorarent exercerentque festiuitatem gentilem. Erat quoque quidam mos apud illos per edictum omnibus intimatus ut quicumque in cunctis regionibus siue procul siue iuxta in illa nocte incendisset ignem antequam in domu regia, id est in palatio Temoriae, succenderetur periret anima eius de populo suo. Santus ergo Patricius sanctum pasca celebrans incendit diuinum ignem ualde lucidum et benedictum, qui in nocte reffulgens a cunctis pene per planitiem campi habitantibus uissus est. Accidit ergo ut a Temoria uideretur uissoque eo conspexerunt omnes et mirati sunt; conuocatisque senioribus regi dixit eis rex: "Quis est qui noc nefas ausus est facere in regno meo? Pereat ille morte!" Et respondentibus omnibus neciisse illum qui hoc fecerit magi responderunt: "Rex, in aeturnum uiue! Hic ignis quem uidemus quique in hac nocte accensus est antequam succenderetur in domu tua nissi extinctus fuerit in nocte hac qua accensus est, numquam extinguetur in aeternum, insuper et omnes ignes nostrae consuitudinis supergradietur, et ille qui incendit et regnum superueniens a quo incensus nocte in hac superabit nos omnes et te et omnes homines regni tui seducet, et cadent ei omnia regna et ipsum inplebit omnia et regnabit in saecula saeculorum."

(1.16) His ergo auditis turbatus est rex Loiguire ualde ut ollim Erodis et omnis ciuitas Temoria cum eo et respondens dixit: "Non sic erit, sed nunc nos ibimus ut uideamus exitum rei, et retinebimus et occidemus facientes tantum nefas in nostrum regnum." Iunctis ergo ter nouem curribus secundum deorum traditionem et assumptis his duobus magis ad conflictionem prae omnibus optimis, id est Lucetmael et Lochru, in fine noctis illius perrexit Loiguire de Temoria ad ferti uirorum Feec, hominum et equorum facies secundum congruum illis sensum ad leuam uertentes. Euntibus autem illis dixerunt magi regi: "Rex, nec tu ibis ad locum in quo ignis est, ne forte tu postea adoraueris illum qui incendit, sed eris foris iuxta et uocabitur ad te ille ut te adorauerit et tu ipse dominatus fueris, et sermocinabimur ad inuicem nos et ille in conspectu tuo, rex, et probabis nos sic," et respondens

all that if anyone near or far who kindled a fire on that night before the king had lit his would lose his life. But holy Patrick lit his sacred Easter fire that night, a blessed a bright fire, that was seen by almost everyone who lived in the plain. Everyone who saw the fire looked on it with wonder. The king called together all his elders and demanded of them, "Who has dared to commit such a crime in my kingdom? Let him be killed!" They all replied that they did not know, but the druids said, "King, may you live forever! This fire which we see, lit on this night before your own, unless it is extinguished tonight it will never be extinguished and will outshine all the fires of our ways. The one who lit it and the rule he brings this night will overcome you and all of us, seducing the people of your kingdom. All our kingdoms will fall before it as it fills the whole land and reigns forever.

(1.16) As formerly with Herod, when King Loíguire heard these things he was greatly troubled and all of Tara with him. He answered and said, "This will not be, but now we will go up and see what is happening. We shall capture and slay those doing these evil deeds in our kingdom." The king ordered three times nine chariots readied, according to the tradition of their gods, and took with him Lucet Máel and Lochru, his two most powerful druids in conflicts. They left Tara at the end of the night towards the burial ground of the men of Fíacc, the faces of men and horses turned to the left as was customary. As they were traveling, the druids said to the Loíguire, "King, do not go yourself to the place where the fire is, lest by chance you might afterwards adore the man who lit it. Instead, stay outside and summon that man to you so that he might adore you and you rule over him. We will then debate that man in your

rex ait: "Bonum consilium inuenistis. Sic faciam ut locuti fuistis." Et peruenierunt ad praefinitum locum, discendentibusque illis de curribus suis et equis non intrauerunt in circuitum loci incensi, sed sederunt iuxta.

(1.17) Et uocatus est sanctus Patricius ad regem extra locum incensi dixeruntque magi ad suos: "Nec surgemus nos in aduentu istius, nam quicumque surrexerit ad aduentum istius credet ei postea et adorabit eum." Surgens denique sanctus Patricius et uidens multos currus et equos eorum huncque psalmistae uersiculum non incongrue in labiis et in corde decantans, "*Hii in curribus et hii in equis, nos autem in nomine Dei nostri ambulabimus*,"[j] uenit ad illos. Illi non surrexerunt in aduentu eius, sed unus tantum a Domino adiuntus qui noluit oboedire dictis magorum, hoc est Ercc filius Dego, cuius nunc reliquae adorantur in illa ciuitate quae uocatur Slane, surrexit et benedixit eum Patricius et credidit Deo aeterno. Incipientibusque illis sermocinari ad inuicem alter magus nomine Lochru procax erat in conspectu sancti audiens detrachere fidei catholicae tumulentis uerbis. Hunc autem intuens turuo oculo talia promentem sanctus Patricius ut quondam Petrus de Simone cum quadam potentia et magno clamore confidenter ad Dominum dixit: "Domine, qui omnia potes et in tua potestate consistunt, quique me missisti huc, hic impius qui blasfemat nomen tuum eleuetur nunc foras et cito moriatur." Et his dictis eliuatus est in aethera magus et iterum dimissus desuper uerso ad lapidem cerebro comminutus et mortuus fuerat coram eis, et timuerant gentiles.

(1.18) Iratusque cum suis rex Patricio super hoc uoluit eum occidere et dixit: "Iniecite manus in istum perdentem nos!" Tunc uidens gentiles impios inruituros in eum sanctus Patricius surrexit claraque uoce dixit: "*Exsurgat Deus et dissipentur inimici eius et fugiant qui oderunt eum a facie eius*."[k] Et statim inruerunt tenebrae et commotio quaedam horribilis et expugnauerunt

j. Ps 19.8 k. Ps 67.2

presence, lord, and you may judge us." The king answered and said, "You give sound advice. I shall do as you have said." They came then to the place and dismounted their horses and chariots, but they did not enter the circle of light, sitting beyond it instead.

(1.17) Thus holy Patrick was summoned to the king outside the light of the fire, while the druids said to themselves, "Let us not rise when he comes, for whoever rises at his coming will afterwards believe in him and adore him." When Patrick came towards them and saw the great number of their chariots and horses, the fitting verse of the psalmist was on his lips and in his heart: "Some come in chariots and some on horses, but we will walk in the name of our God." They did not rise at his approach, except for one who was prompted by the Lord not to obey the orders of the druids. This was Ercc, son of Daig, whose relicts are now adored in that town called Slane. He rose and Patrick blessed him, and he believed in the eternal God. The debate then began with one of the druids named Lochru provoking holy Patrick and reviling the universal faith with vile words. As he said such things, Patrick looked him in the eye and—just as Peter had once done with Simon—spoke to the Lord with confident and powerful words: "Lord, you who have power over everything and whose power holds together all things, you who sent me here, lift up this impious man who blasphemes your name, cast him out, and let him die a speedy death." At these words the magician was lifted up into the air and fell down again, splitting open his skull on a rock. He died in front of everyone, and the pagans were filled with fear.

(1.18) The king and those with him were so furious at Patrick's action that they wished to kill him. The king shouted: "Grab this man who is destroying us!" When holy Patrick saw that these wicked pagans were about to attack him he said with a loud voice: "Let God rise up, may his enemies be scattered, and may those who hate him flee from his face." Immediately darkness fell and a horrible

impii semet ipsos alter aduersus alterum insurgens et terraemotus magnus factus est et collocauit axes curruum eorum et agebat eos cum ui et praecipitauerunt se currus et equi per planitiem campi donec ad extremum pauci ex eis semiuiui euasserunt ad montem Monduirn, et prostrati sunt ab hac plaga coram rege ex suis sermonibus ad maledictum Patricii septem septies uiri donec ipse remanserat quattuor tantum hominibus, ipse et uxor eius et alii ex Scotis duo, et timuerunt ualde. Veniensque regina ad Patriciam dixit ei: "Homo iuste et potens, ne perdas regem; ueniens enim rex genua flectet et adorabit dominum tuum." Et uenit rex timore coactus et flexit genua coram sancto et finxit adorare quem nolebat; et postquam separauerunt ad inuicem paululum gradiens uocabit rex sanctum Patricium simulato uerbo uolens interficere eum quo modo. Sciens autem Patricius cogitationes regis pessimi benedictis in nomine Iesu Christi sociis suis octo uiris cum puero uenit ad regem ac numerauit eos rex uenientes statimque nusquam conparuerunt ab oculis regis, sed uiderunt gentiles octo tantum ceruos cum hynulo euntes quasi ad dissertum, et rex Loiguire mestus, timidus et ignominiossus cum paucis euadentibus ad Temoriam uersus est deluculo.

(1.19) Sequenti uero die, hoc est in die pascae, recumbentibus regibus et principibus et magis apud Loiguire—festus enim dies maximus apud eos erat—manducantibus illis et bibentibus uinum in palatio Temoriae sermocinantibusque aliis et aliis cogitantibus de his quae facta fuerant, sanctus Patricius quinque tantum uiris, ut contenderet et uerbum faceret de fide sancta in Temoria coram omnibus nationibus, hostiis claussis secundum id quod de Christo legitur uenit. Adueniente ergo eo in caenacolum Temoriae nemo de omnibus ad aduentum eius surrexit praeter unum tantum, id est Dubthoch maccu Lugir, poetam optimum, apud quem tunc temporis ibi erat quidam adoliscens poeta nomine Feec, qui postea mirabilis episcopus fuit, cuius reliquiae adorantur hi Sleibti; hic, ut dixi, Dubthach solus ex gentibus in honorem

commotion arose as these wicked men fought among themselves. A great earthquake struck and the axles of their chariots smashed against each other. Their horses and chariots were driven violently forward through the plain until only a few of the men, half-alive, escaped to Mount Monduirn. Before the eyes of the king seven times seven men perished because of the king's own words. The only four who remained alive were the king, his wife, and two other Irishmen, and they were all very afraid. The queen came to Patrick and said: "O just and powerful man, do not destroy the king. He is coming to you on bended knee to adore your Lord." The king, driven by fear, then came forward and fell on his knees before the holy man to adore him, but he did not wish to. Then after he had gone a little ways from Patrick the king called the holy man to him with feigned kindness wishing in truth to kill him. But Patrick knew what the evil king had in mind. After blessing his companions, eight men and a boy, in the name of Jesus Christ, they began to walk towards the king. Loíguire counted them as they approached but suddenly they disappeared from before his eyes. All he saw were eight deer and a fawn going as if to the wilderness. Loíguire was then sad, fearful, and greatly shamed as he returned to Tara with those few who had escaped Patrick's curse.

(1.19) On the following day, which was Easter, the kings, princes, and druids were all feasting with Loíguire, for this was the day of their greatest festival. They were eating and drinking wine in the palace at Tara, while some were talking and others thinking about the things that had happened. Suddenly holy Patrick and five of his companions entered through closed doors, just as it is said of Christ, so that he might preach and demonstrate the sacred faith at Tara before all peoples. As he entered the dining hall of Tara no one arose to welcome him except one man, Dubthach maccu Lugir, the greatest poet. With him was a young man named Fíacc who at that time was still a boy, but afterwards he became a famous bishop whose relics are adored at Sléibte. This Dubthach, as I have said, was the only one to rise in honor of holy Patrick. The holy man blessed him and on

sancti Patricii surrexit et benedixit ei sanctus credidit que primus in illa die Deo et *repputatum est ei ad iustitiam*.[l] Visso itaque Patricio uocatus est a gentibus ad uescendum, ut probarent eum in uenturis rebus. Ille autem *sciens quae uentura essent*[m] non reffellit uesci.

(1.20) Caenantibus autem omnibus ille magus Lucetmail, qui fuerat in nocturna conflictione, etiam in illa die solicitus est extincto consocio suo confligere aduersus sanctum Patricium, et ut initium causae haberet, intuentibus aliis inmissit aliquid ex uasse suo in poculum Patricii, ut probaret quid faceret. Vidensque sanctus Patricius hoc probationis genus uidentibus cunctis benedixit poculum suum et uersus est liquor in modum gelu et conuerso uasse cicidit gutta illa tantum quam inmisserat magus, et iterum benedixit poculum, conuersus est liquor in naturam suam et mirati sunt omnes. Et post paululum ait magus: "Faciamus signa super hunc campum maximum" respondensque Patricius ait: "Quae?," et dixit magus: "Inducamus niuem super terram," et ait Patricius: "Nolo contraria uoluntati Dei inducere," et dixit magus: "Ego inducam uidentibus cunctis." Tunc incantationes magicas exorsus induxit niuem super totum campum pertinguentum ferenn et uiderunt omnes et mirati sunt. Et ait sanctus: "Ecce uidemus hoc, depone nunc." Et dixit: "Ante istam horam cras non possum deponere." Et ait sanctus: "Potes malum et non bonum facere. Non sic ego." Tunc benedicens per totum circuitum campum dicto citius absque ulla pluia aut nebulis aut uento euanuit nix, et exclamauerunt turbae et mirati sunt ualde et compuncti sunt corde. Et paulo post inuocatis demonibus induxit magus densissimas tenebras super terram in signum et mormurauerunt omnes. Et ait sanctus: "Expelle tenebras." At ille similiter non poterat. Sanctus autem orans benedixit et reppente expulsae sunt tenebrae at refulsit sol et exclamauerunt omnes et gratias egerunt. His autem omnibus gestis in conspectu regis inter magum Patriciumque ait rex ad illos: "Libros uestros in aquam

l. Gn 15.6 m. Jn 18.4

that day he was the first to believe in God, and "it was counted unto him as righteousness." When the pagans saw Patrick, they asked him to eat with them so that they might test him later. And Patrick, "knowing what was going to happen," did not refuse their invitation.

(1.20) While they were all eating, one of the druids named Lucet Máel, who had taken part in the conflict the previous night in which his comrade had been killed, was eager on that day to challenge holy Patrick. To begin he put a drop of poison from his cup into Patrick's cup while everyone watched to see what would happen. When Patrick saw how he was being tested, he blessed his cup as all looked on and the liquid froze like ice. He then turned the cup upside down and only the drop the magician had added fell out. He then blessed the cup again and the liquid melted into its natural state while everyone was amazed. After a little while the magician said: "Let us perform wonders on this vast plain." And Patrick said: "What kind of wonders?" And the magician said: "Let us call down snow over the land." And Patrick said: "I do not want to do anything contrary to the will of God." And the magician said: "I will bring down snow for everyone to see." Then he uttered magical spells and called down snow over the whole plain up to the depth of a man's belt,[25] and everyone was amazed. The holy man said: "We have seen what you can do. Now remove the snow." The magician said: "I cannot remove it until this same time tomorrow." And the holy man said: "You can work evil, but not good. Not so with me." He then blessed the whole field and—without rain, mist or wind—the snow disappeared in an instant. The crowd cheered and were touched in their hearts. A little while later, the magician, by calling on demons, called down darkness on the whole land as a wonder, and the people muttered angrily. The holy man said: "Remove the darkness." But again the magician was not able. The holy man however said a prayer and drove away the darkness. The sun shone and everyone shouted with gladness and thanks.

25. *ferenn*: Old Irish "belt."

mittite et illum cuius libri inlessi euasserunt adorabimus." Respondit Patricius: "Faciam ego," et dixit magus: "Nolo ego ad iudicium aquae uenire cum isto; aquam enim deum habet;" certe audiuit babtisma per aquam a Patricio datum. Et respondens rex ait: "Permitte per ignem." Et ait Patricius: "Prumptus sum." At magus nolens dixit: "Hic homo uersa uice in alternos annos nunc aquam nunc ignem deum ueneratur." Et ait sanctus: "Non sic, sed tu ipse ibis et unus ex meis pueris ibit tecum in separatam et conclaussam domum et meum erga te et tuum erga meum puerum erit uestimentum et sic simul incendemini et iudicabimini in conspectu Altissimi." Et hoc concilium insedit et aedificata est eis domus cuius dimedium ex materia uiridi et alterum dimedium ex arida facta est, et missus est magus in illam domum in partem eius uiridem et unus ex pueris sancti Patricii Benineus nomine cum ueste magica in partem domus aridam; conclussa itaque extrinsecus domus coram omni turba incensa est. Et factum est illa hora orante Patricio ut consumeret flamma ignis magum cum demedia domu uiridi permanente cassula sancti Patricii tantum intacta, quam ignis non tetigit. Felix autem Benineus e contrario cum demedia domu arida, secundum quod de tribus pueris dictum est, *non tetigit eum ignis omnino neque contristatus est nec quicquam molestiae intulit,*[n] cassula tantum magi quae erga eum fuerat non sine Dei nutu exusta. Et iratus est ualde rex aduersus Patricium de morte magi sui et inruit poene in eum uolens occidere, sed prohibuit illum Deus. Ad praecem enim Patricii et ad uocem eius discendit ira Dei in populum inpium et perierunt multi ex eis. Et ait sanctus Patricius regi: "Nisi nunc credideris cito morieris, quia discendet ira Dei in uerticem tuum." Et timuit rex uehimenter et commotum est cor eius et omnis ciuitas cum eo.

(1.21) Congregatis igitur senioribus et omni senatu suo dixit eis rex Loiguire: "Melius est credere me quam mori," initoque

n. Dn 3.50

After all these contests between the magician and Patrick in the sight of the king, the king said: "Throw your books into the water. I will worship the man whose book is not damaged." Patrick responded: "I will do it." But the magician said: "I do not wish to be judged by water with this man, for water is a god to him." He had apparently heard that Patrick baptized with water. The king therefore said: "Send the books through fire." Patrick said: "I am ready." But the magician refused saying: "This man worships fire and water in alternate years." And the holy man said: "That is not true. But you and one of the boys with me go into an enclosed house divided in two parts. You wear my vestment while my boy wears your robe. Then both of you shall be set on fire and be judged in the sight of the Most High." This was agreed upon and they built a house with half green wood and half dry wood. The magician went into the green part while one of Patrick's boys named Benineus[26] went into the part made of dry wood wearing the druids robe. The house was then closed up and set on fire while the whole crowd watched. Thus it happened in that hour that through Patrick's prayers the flames consumed the magician and the green wood of the house completely. Only Patrick's chasuble survived untouched by the fire. The opposite happened to happy Benineus. Although he was in the dry part of the structure, it was as it is said of the three young men: "The fire did not touch him at all and caused him no pain or distress." Only the magician's robe was burnt, according to God's will. The king was greatly angered at Patrick concerning the magician's death and would have killed him, but was prevented by God. For by the prayer of Patrick and by his word the anger of God descended on those wicked people, and many of them perished. Holy Patrick then said to the king: "Unless you now believe, you will quickly die, for the anger of God has come upon your head." And the king was very afraid. His heart was in great turmoil and all the city with him.

(1.21) Therefore King Loíguire summoned his elders and all his advisors to him and said: "It is better for me to believe than die."

26. *Benineus*: Benignus (cf. Tírechán 8 and Muirchú 1.25 below).

consilio ex suorum praecepto credidit in illa die et conuertit ad Dominum Deum aeternum, et ibi crediderunt multi alii. Et ait sanctus Patricius ad regem: "Quia restitisti doctrinae meae et fuisti scandalum mihi, licet prolonguentur dies regni tui, nullus tamen erit ex semine tuo rex in aeternum."

(1.22) Sanctus autem Patricius secundum praeceptum Domini Iesu *iens et docens omnes gentes babtitzansque eas in nomine Patris et Filii et Spiritus Sancti*[o] *profectus* a Temoria *praedicauit ubique Domino cooperante et sermonem confirmante sequentibus signis.*[p]

(1.27) Itaque uolente Domino Patricii, ut ita dicam totius Hiberniae episcopi doctorisque egregii, de uirtutibius pauca pluribus enarrare conabor. Quodam igitur tempore cum tota Britannia incredulitatis algore rigesceret cuiusdam regis egregia filia, cui nomen erat Monesan, Spiritu Sancto repleta, cum quidam eius expeterent amplexus coniugalis non adquieuit cum aquarum multis irrigata esset undis ad id quod nolebat et deterius erat conpelli potuit. Nam illa cum inter uerbera et aquarum irrigationes solita esset interrogabat matrem et nutricem utrum conpertum haberent rotae factorem qua totus illuminatur mundus, et cum responsum acciperet solis factorem esse eum cui caelum sedes est, cum acta esset frequenter ut coniugali uinculo copularetur, luculentissimo Spiritus Sancti illustrata: "Nequaquam," inquit, "hoc faciam." Quaerebat namque per naturam totius creaturae factorem in hoc patriarchae Abraham secuta exemplum. Parentes eius initio consilio ado iusti tributo audito Patricio uiro ab aeterno Deo uisitato septimo semper die Scoticas partes cum filia pulsauere Patriciumque tanto labore quaesitum reperire; qui illos nouicios percunctari caepit. Tunc illi uiatores clamare ceperunt et dicere: "Cupidissimae filiae uidendi Deum causa coacti ad te uenire facti sumus." Tunc ille repletus Spiritu Sancto eleuauit uocem suam et dixit ad eam: "Si in Deum credis?" Et ait: "Credo." Tunc sacro Spiritus et aquae lauacro eam lauit. Nec mora, post ea solo

o. Mt 28.19 p. Mk 16.20

Having held this meeting, he consented to the advice of his men and on that day converted to the eternal Lord God, and many others believed as well. Holy Patrick then said to him: "Because you resisted my teachings and were an obstacle to me, the days of your own reign shall continue, but none of your descendants shall ever be king."

(1.22) Then holy Patrick, according to the teachings of the Lord Jesus, left Tara and "went forth and taught all people, baptizing them in the name of the Father and of the Son and of the Holy Spirit." "He preached everywhere with the Lord helping by confirming his words by miracles that followed."

(1.27) With the Lord willing, I will try to relate a few of the wonders done by Patrick, who, if I may say so, was the bishop and teacher of all Ireland. At that time when all Britain was frozen in unbelief, there was a certain remarkable daughter of a king, and her name was Monesan. She was filled with the Holy Spirit, who helped her not to give in to those who sought to marry her. Even though she was frequently drenched with water she would not consent to what she believed was wrong and less worthy. In between beating and drenching to persuade her to marry, she kept asking her mother and nurse who had made the spheres of heaven that illuminated the world. When she was told that the maker of the sun was he whose seat is in heaven, she, though repeatedly urged to take on the bonds of marriage, was urged by the Holy Spirit to say: "Never will I do this." For she was seeking through nature the maker of all creation just as Abraham had done. Her parents were considering what to do when they heard that Patrick was a just man who was visited by God every seventh day. They then took their daughter to Ireland to look for Patrick and with great effort found him. He asked them why they had come and they answered: "The burning desire of our daughter to see God is why we have come to you." Then Patrick, filled with the Holy Spirit, lifted up his voice and said to the woman: "Do you believe in God?" And she replied: "I do." Then he washed her with water and the Holy Spirit. Immediately she fell down to the ground

prostrata spiritum in manus angelorum tradidit. Ubi moritur ibi et adunatur. Tunc Patricius prophetauit quod post annos uiginti corpus illius ad propinquam cellulam de illo loco tolleretur cum honore. Quod postea ita factum est. Cuius transmarinae reliquiae ibi adorantur usque hodie.

(1.29) Quoddam mirabile gestum Patricii non transibo silentio. Huic nauntiatum est nequissimum opus cuiusdam regis Britannici nomine Corictic infausti crudelisque tyrranni. Hic namque erat maximus persecutor interfectorque Christianorum. Patricius autem per epistolam ad uiam ueritatis reuocare temptauit; cuius salutaria deridebat monita. Cum autem ita nuntiaretur Patricio orauit Dominum et dixit: "Domine, si fieri potest, expelle hunc perfidum de praesenti saeculoque futuro." Non grande post ea tempus effluxerat et musicam artem audiuit a quodam cantare quod de solio regali transiret, omnesque karissimi eius uiri in hanc proruperunt uocem. Tunc ille cum esset in medio foro, ilico uulpiculi miserabiliter arepta forma profectus in suorum praesentia ex illo die illaque hora uelut fluxus aquae transiens nusquam conparuit.

(1.28) Dominici et apostolici Patricii, cuius mentionem facimus, quoddam miraculum mirifice gestum in carne adhuc stanti quod ei et Stephano poene tantum contigisse legitur, breui retexam relatu. Quodam ante tempore cum orationis causa ad locum solitum per nocturna spacia procideret consueta, caeli uidit miracula, suumque carissimum ac fidelem probare uolens sanctum puerum dixit: "O fili mi, dic michi, quaeso, si sentis ea quae sentio." Tunc paruulus nomine Benignus incunctanter dixit: "Iam michi cognita ea quae sentis. Nam uideo caelum apertum et filium Dei et angelos eius." Tunc Patricius dixit: "Iam te meum successorem dignum esse sentio." Nec mora, gradu consito ad consuetum locum orationis peruenire. His orationibus in medio fluminis alueo paruulus dixit: "Iam algorem aquaticum sustinere non possum." Nam ei aqua nimis erat frigida. Tunc dixit ei Patricius

dead and gave her spirit into the hands of the angels. She was then buried where she had died. Patrick then prophesied that after twenty years her body would be carried from that place to a nearby chapel. And thus it was done. The relics of the woman from across the sea are adored there to this day.

(1.29) I cannot pass over in silence another of Patrick's amazing deeds. News had come to him of the wicked actions of a certain king of the Britons named Corotic, a cruel and foul tyrant.[27] He was also a great persecutor and murderer of Christians. Patrick had written a letter to him to try and call him back to the way of truth, but Corotic only laughed at him. When Patrick was told of this he prayed to God and said: "Lord, if it is possible, expel this traitor from your presence now and forever." Not long after this Corotic heard music and someone singing that he should leave his throne. Then all those dearest to him burst into this same song. Then Corotic suddenly and in the middle of his hall was shamefully changed into a fox and ran off. Since that time, like water that has flowed away, he was never seen again.

(1.28) I must briefly mention another deed that godly and apostolic man Patrick accomplished while he was still in the flesh. This deed is only written of him and Stephen. Once when he was going to his usual place to pray alone at night, he saw the wonders of heaven. Wishing to test his beloved and faithful holy boy, he said to him: "O my son, please tell me if you see what I see." Then the boy, named Benignus, said to him right away: "I know what you sense, for I see heaven open and the son of God and his angels." Then Patrick said: "Now I know that you are worthy to be my successor." They walked quickly and came to Patrick's usual place of prayer. While they were praying there in the middle of a stream bed, the boy said: "I am not able to bear this cold water." For the water was too cold. Then Patrick told him to go from the upper part of the stream to the lower. But there too he was unable to remain long for, as he admitted, the

27. Corotic was the British tyrant Coroticus of Patrick's *Letter*.

ut de superiori ad inferiorem descenderet. Nichilominus ibi diu perstare potuit. Nam se aquam nimis calidam sensisse testabatur. Tunc ille non sustinens in eo loco diu stare terram ascendit.

(1.23) Erat quidam homo in regionibus Ulothorum Patricii tempore, Macuil moccu Greccae, et erat hic homo ualde impius saeuus tyrannus, ut cyclops nominaretur, cogitationibus prauus, uerbis intemperatus, factis malignus, spiritu amarus, anima iracondus, corpore scelestus, mente crudelis, uita gentilis, conscientia inanis, in tantum uergens impietatis in profundum ita ut die quadam in montosso aspero altoque sedens loco hi nDruim moccu Echach, ubi ille tyrannidem cotidie exercebat signa sumens nequissima crudelitatis et transeuntes hospites crudeli scelere interficiens, sanctum quoque Patricium claro fidei lumine radiantem et miro quodam caelestis gloriae deademate fulgentem uidens cum inconcussa doctrinae fiducia per congruum uiae iter ambulantem interficere cogitaret dicens satilitibus suis: "Ecce seductor ille et peruersor hominum uenit, cui mos facere praestigias, ut decipiat homines multosque seducat. Eamus ergo et temptemus eum et sciemus si habet potentiam aliquam ille deus in quo se glorietur." Temptaueruntque uirum sanctum hoc modo: Posuerunt unum ex semet ipsis sanum in medio eorum sub sago iacentem infirmitatemque mortis simulantem, ut probarent sanctum in huiusque modi fallaci re, sanctum seductorem, uirtutis praestigias et orationes ueneficia uel incantationes nominantes. Adueniente ergo sancto Patricio cum discipulis suis gentiles dixerunt ei: "Ecce unus ex nobis nunc infirmatus est; accede itaque et canta super eum alias incantationes sectae tuae, si forte sanari possit." Sanctus autem Patricius sciens omnes dolos et fallacias eorum constanter et intripide ait: "Nec mirum si infirmus fuisset," et reuelantes socii eius faciem simulantis infirmitatem uiderunt eum iam mortuum. At illi obstupescentes ammirantesque tale miraculum dixerunt intra se gentes: "Vere hic homo Dei est; malefecimus temptantes eum." Sanctus uero Patricius conuersus ad Maccuil ait: "Quare temptare me uoluisti?"

water was too warm. Then unable to stay in that place he climbed up onto land.

(1.23) In the days of Patrick there was a man of the Ulaid region named Macc Cuill moccu Graccae. This man was a wicked and savage tyrant, so much so that he was called the Cyclops. He was depraved in his thoughts, intemperate in his words, wicked in his deeds, bitter in his spirit, angry in his temper, sinful in his body, cruel in his mind, a pagan in his life, and foolish in his conscience. He had sunk so low in wickedness that one day while he was sitting on a wild, high hill in Druim moccu Echach—where he daily exercised his tyranny, wearing the signs of his harsh cruelty, murdering travelers as they passed by—he saw holy Patrick approaching, shining as it were with the clear light of faith and the crown of heavenly glory, making his way along with the untroubled trust that came from his teaching. The outlaw then said to his evil companions: "Look, there is the man who seduces and misleads people. He performs his tricks to deceive people and lead them astray. Let's go and test him so that we can find out if this god in whom he glories has any power." This is how they tested the holy man—they placed one of their number, who was in perfectly good health, in the middle of them under a cloak and pretended he was deathly ill. They did this to prove the holy man was a fraud, to show he was a seducer, to reveal his wonders as deceptions, and to label his prayers as evil incantations. So as Patrick and his disciples approached, the pagans said to him: "Look, one of our number is sick. Come and sing some of the incantations of your sect over him that he might be well." Holy Patrick knew all their evil deeds and tricks, firmly and fearlessly said to them: "His condition would be no surprise if he had truly been sick." They then uncovered the face of their companion feigning illness and saw that he was dead. The pagans were astonished and bewildered by such a wonder and said among themselves: "Truly this is a man of God. It was evil of us to test him." Holy Patrick then turned to Macc Cuill and said: " Why did you want to test me?" That cruel tyrant then

respondensque ille tyrannus crudelis ait: “Poenitet me facti huius, et quodcumque praeceperis mihi faciam, et trado me nunc in potentiam dei tui excelsi quem praedicas.” Et ait sanctus: “Crede ergo in Deo meo Domino Iesu et confitere peccata tua et babtitzare in nomine Patris et Filii et Spiritus Sancti.” Et conuersus in illa hora credidit Deo aeterno babtitzatusque est; insuper et haec addidit Maccuill dicens: “Confiteor tibi, sancte domine mi Patrici, quia proposui te interficere; iudica ergo quantum debuerit pro tanto ac tali cremine.” Et ait Patricius: “Non possum iudicare, sed Deus iudicabit. Tu tamen egredire nunc inermis ad mare et transi uelociter de regione hac Hibernensi nihil tollens tecum de tua substantia praeter uile et paruum indumentum quo possit corpus tantum contegi, nihil gustans nihilque bibens de fructu insolae huius, habens hoc insigne peccati tui in capite tuo, et postquam peruenias ad mare conliga pedes tuos conpede ferreo et proiece clauim eius in mari et mitte te in nauim unius pellis absque gubernaculo et absque remo, et quocumque te duxerit uentus et mare esto paratus et terram in quamcumque defferat te diuina prouidentia inhabita et exerce ibi diuina mandata.” Dixitque Maccuill: “Sic faciam ut dixisti. De uiro autem mortuo quid faciemus?” Et ait Patricius: “Viuet et exsurget sine dolore.” Et suscitauit eum Patricius in illa hora, et reuixit sanus. Et migrauit inde Maccuil ad mare dexteram campi Inis habeta fiducia inconcussa fidei collegauitque se in litore ieciens clauim in mare secundum quod praeceptum est ei, et ascendit mare in nauicula et inspirauit illi uentus aquilo et sustulit eum ad meridiem iecitque eum in insolam Euoniam nomine, inuenitque ibi duo uiros ualde mirabiles in fide et doctrina fulgentes, qui primi docuerunt uerbum Dei et babtismum in Euonia et conuersi sunt homines insolae in doctrina eorum ad fidem catholicam, quorum nomina sunt Conindri et Rumili. Hii uero uidentes uirum unius habitus mirati sunt et miserti sunt illius eliuaueruntque de mari suscipientes cum gaudio. Ille igitur ubi inuenti sunt spiritales patres in regione a Deo sibi credita ad regulam eorum corpus et animam exercuit et totum

said: "I repent that I did this to you. Whatever you require of me I will do. I give myself over now to the power of your high god whom you preach." The holy one then said: "Believe therefore in my God the Lord Jesus and be baptized in the name of the Father and Son and Holy Spirit." Macc Cuill turned that hour to the eternal God and was baptized. Then Macc Cuill continued: "I confess to you, my holy lord Patrick, that I had planned to murder you. Judge therefore what price I should pay for such a great crime." And Patrick said: "I am not able to judge you, but God will judge. Go therefore down to the seashore unarmed and quickly leave this part of Ireland taking nothing with you from your goods except a worn garment that barely covers your body. Don't eat or drink anything of the fruit of this island with a mark of your sins upon your head. When you come to the sea bind your feet in an iron fetter and throw the key into the waves. Then set off to sea in a boat only one skin thick without a rudder or oar. Be prepared to go to whatever land the winds and sea will take you. Wherever divine providence sends you, there live and obey the divine commands." And Macc Cuill answered: "I will do as you have said. But what should we do about this dead man?" And Patrick said: "He will live and rise without pain." In that same hour Patrick raised him from the dead and he returned to health. Macc Cuill then left and with the confidence of certain faith went to the shore south of Mag Inis. He fettered his feet and threw the key into the sea as he had been instructed. He then climbed into the little boat and set out. The north wind blew him to the south until he came to an island called Euonia.[28] There he found two excellent men splendid in faith and teaching. They had been the first to teach the word of God in Euonia and by their teaching had converted the people of the island to the universal faith. Their names were Conindrus and Rumilus. These two were amazed when saw the man dressed as he was and had pity on him. They brought him from the sea and embraced him with joy. He therefore having found spiritual fathers in a place appointed to him by God trained his body and

28. *Euonia* is identified with the Isle of Man.

uitae tempus ibi exegit apud istos duos sanctos episcopus usque dum successor eorum in episcopatu effectus est. Hic est Maccuill di Mane episcopus et antestes Arddae Huimnonn.

(1.25) Alia uero uice sanctus requiescens Patricius in die dominica supra mare iuxta salsuginem quae est ad aquilonalem plagem a Collo Bouis distans non magno uiae spatio audiuit sonum intemperatum gentilium in die dominica laborantium facientium fossam rathi. Vocatisque illis prohibuit eos Patricius ne laborarent in dominico die. At illi non consentiebant uerbis sancti, quin immo inridentes deludebant eum. Et ait sanctus Patricius: "Mudebroth, quamuis laboraueritis nec tamen proficiat." Quod conpletum est. Insequenti enim nocte uentus magnus adueniens turbauit mare et omne opus gentilium distruxit tempestas iuxta uerbum sancti.

(1.24) Fuit quidam homo diues et honorabilis in regionibus orientalium cui nomen erat Daire. Hunc autem rogauit Patricius ut aliquem locum ad exercendam religionem daret ei, dixitque diues ad sanctum: "Quem locum petis?" "Peto," inquit sanctus, "ut illam altitudinem terrae quae nominatur Dorsum Salicis dones mihi, et construam ibi locum." At ille noluit sancto terram illam dare altam, sed dedit illi locum alium in inferiori terra, ubi nunc est fertae martyrum iuxta Ardd Mache, et habitauit ibi sanctus Patricius cum suis. Post uero aliquod tempus uenit eques Dairi ducens equum suum, ut pasceretur in herbosso loco Christianorum, et offendit Patricium talis dilatio equi in locum suum et ait: "Stulte fecit Daire bruta mittens animalia turbare locum paruum quem dedit Deo." At uero eques tamquam *sordus non audiebat et sicut mutus non aperiens os suum*[q] nihil loquebatur, sed dimisso ibi equo nocte illa exiuit. Crastino autem die mane ueniens eques uissitare equum suum inuenit eum iam mortuum domique reuersus tristis ait ad dominum suum: "Ecce Christianus ille occidit equum tuum; offendit enim illum turbatio loci sui," et dixit Daire:

q. Ps 37.14

spirit to obey their rule. He spent the rest of his life there with these two holy bishops until he became their successor as bishop. This is Macc Cuill, bishop of Mane and prelate of Arde Huimnonn.

(1.25) On another occasion, holy Patrick was resting on a Sunday beside a marsh on the seashore not far north of Druimm Bó. There he heard the loud noise of some pagans digging a ditch on Sunday around a fort. Calling them, he ordered them not to work on the Lord's day, but they ignored the words of the holy man and even laughed at him. Then holy Patrick said: "Mudebroth![29] All your work will gain you nothing." And thus it happened just as the holy man said. On the following night a great wind arose and stirred up the waves destroying all the work of the pagans.

(1.24) There was once a wealthy and honored man in the eastern regions whose name was Dáire. Patrick asked him if he would give him some land to practice his religion, and the rich man said to the holy man: "What land do you want?" The holy man said: "I would like you to give to me that high piece of land that is called Druimm Sailech so I can build on it." But he did not want to give the holy man the high ground, so he granted him another piece of land on the low ground where there is now the burial ground of martyrs near Armagh. There holy Patrick settled with his followers. Some time later a man who looked after Dáire's horses brought one of the animals there to let it graze in the meadow of the Christians. Patrick was offended by the release of the horse in his piece of land and said to the servant: "Dáire has behaved foolishly by sending a brute animal to disturb this place he gave to God." But the servant, saying nothing "as if he were deaf and like one who is mute who does not open his mouth," went away and left the horse there for the night. But the next day the servant came to see to the horse and found it dead. He sadly returned to his master's house and said to him:

29. *Mudebroth* (also *Mudebrod*) is an Irish corruption of an early British phrase meaning "by the God of judgment."

"Occidatur et ille; nunc ite et interficite eum." Euntibus autem illis foras dictu citius repentina inruit mors super Daire, et ait uxor eius: "Caussa Christiani est haec mors. Eat quis cito et portentur nobis beneficia eius et saluus eris, et prohibenter et reuocentur qui exierunt ad Christianum occidere eum." Exieruntque duo uiri, qui dixerunt ei celantes quod factum est: "Ecce infirmatus est Daire; portetur illi aliquid a te si forte sanari possit." Sanctus autem Patricius sciens quae facta sunt dixit: "Nimirum," benedixitque aquam et dedit eis dicens: "Ite aspargite equum uestrum ex aqua ista et portate illam uobiscum." Et fecerunt sic et reuixit equus, et portauerunt secum sanatusque est Daire asparsione aquae sanctae. Et uenit Daire post haec ut honoraret sanctum Patricium, portans secum eneum mirabilem transmarinum metritas ternas capientem, dixitque Daire ad sanctum: "Ecce hic aeneus sit tecum," et ait sanctus Patricius "Grazacham." Reuersusque Daire ad domum suam dixit: "Stultus homo est, qui nihil boni dixit praeter 'Grazacham' tantum pro aeneo mirabili metritarum trium," additque Daire dicens seruis suis: "Ite reportate nobis aeneum nostrum." Exierunt et dixerunt Patricio: "Portabimus aeneum." Nihilominus et illa uice sanctus Patricius dixit: "Grazacham, portate," et portauerunt. Interrogauitque Daire socios suos dicens: "Quid dixit Christianus quando reportastis aeneum?" At illi responderunt: " 'Grazacham' dixit." Et ille respondens dixit" " 'Grazacham' in dato, 'Grazacham' in ablato. Eius dictum tam bonum est; cum 'Grazacham' illis portabitur illi rursum aeneus suus." Et uenit Daire ipsemet illa uice et portauit aeneum ad Patricium dicens ei: "Fiat tecum aeneus tuus. Constans enim et incommotabilis homo es. Insuper et partem illam agri quam ollim petisti do tibi nunc quantum habeo, et in habita ibi." Et illa est ciuitas quae nunc Ardd Machae nominatur. Et exierunt ambo sanctus Patricius et Daire ut considerarent mirabile oblationis et beneplacitum munus, et ascenderunt illam altitudinem terrae inuenieruntque ceruuam cum uitulo suo paruo iacente in

"Look, that Christian killed your horse because it offended him to have that placed disturbed." And Dáire said to his men: "That man must die. Go now and kill him." But just as the men were going out, death came upon Dáire. His wife then said: "The Christian is the cause of this death. Someone go quickly to seek his blessings and you will be well. Call back also those who went out to kill the Christian." Two men then went out and spoke to Patrick, concealing what had happened: "Look, Dáire is sick. Give us something to bring to him that he might be well." But holy Patrick, knowing all that had happened, said to them: "Oh really?" Then he blessed some water and gave it to them saying: "Go and sprinkle this on your horse, then take the animal with you." They did this and the horse came back to life. Then when they sprinkled the water on Dáire he was revived as well. After this Dáire came to honor holy Patrick and brought as a gift an amazing bronze cauldron from overseas which held three measures. Dáire said to the holy man: "Behold, this bronze cauldron is yours." And holy Patrick said: "Thanks."[30] Dáire went home and said to his household: "This man is a fool. I gave him a wonderful bronze cauldron capable of holding three measures and all he says is 'Thanks.'" Dáire then said to his servants: "Go and bring my cauldron back." They went out and said to Patrick: "We are taking the cauldron back." But Patrick then simply said: "Thanks. Take it away." And they did so. Dáire asked his men: "What did the Christian say when you took back the cauldron?" And they answered: "He said 'Thanks.'" Dáire then said: "'Thanks' for giving and 'Thanks' for taking away. This is such a good response that because of his 'Thanks' he shall receive his cauldron back again." And Dáire himself returned to Patrick immediately with the cauldron and said to him: " This cauldron is yours to keep since you are a steady and imperturbable man. Moreover I now give to you that piece of land you first requested that you may live there." There is the city now called Armagh. Then both Patrick and Dáire went out to inspect the wonderful and pleasing gift. On top of the hill they found a doe with

30. *Grazacham* is a colloquial form of *gratias agamus* ("we give thanks").

loco in quo nunc altare est sinistralis aeclessiae in Ardd Machae, et uoluerunt comites Patricii tenere uitulum et occidere, sed noluit sanctus neque permissit, quin potius ipsemet sanctus tenuit uitulum portans eum in humeris suis, et secuta illum cerua uelut amantissimaque ouis usque dum dimisserat uitulum in altero saltu ad aquilonalem plagam Airdd Mache, ubi usque hodie signa quaedam uirtutis esse manentia periti dicunt.

(1.26) Virum aliquem ualde durum et tam auarum in campo Inis habitantem in tantum stultitiae auaritiaeque incurrisse cremen periti ferunt ut duos boues carram Patricii uechentes alio die post sanctum laborem in pastu agili sui requiescentibus pascentibusque se bobus uiolenter praesente sancto Patricio uanus ille homo per uim coegit. Cui irascens sanctus Patricius cum maledictione dixit: "Mudebrod, male fecisti. Nusquam proficiat tibi ager hic tuus neque semini tuo in aeternum; iam inutilis erit." Et factum est sic: inundatio etenim maris tam habunda eodem ueniens die circumluit et operuit totum agrum, et possitus est iuxta profetae uerbum: *terra fructifera in salsuginem a malitia inhabitantis in ea.*[r] Arenossa ergo et infructuossa haec a die qua maledixit eam sanctus Patricius usque in hodiernum diem.

Liber Secundus

(1) De Patricii deligentia orationis
(2) De mortuo ad se loquente
(3) De inluminata dominica nocte, ut equi inuenti sunt
(4) De eo quod angelus eum prohibuit ne i Machi moriretur
(5) De rubo ardente in qua erat angelus
(6) De quattuor Patricii petitionibus
(7) De die mortis eius et de tempore uitae cxx annorum
(8) De termino contra noctem possito et de caligne duodecim noctium abstersa

r. Ps 106.34

her small fawn lying there in the place where now is the altar of the northern church at Armagh. The companions of Patrick wanted to capture and kill the fawn, but the holy man told them not to. He took up the fawn and carried it on his shoulders while the doe followed him meekly like a loving lamb to a nearby meadow north of Armagh. There, as wise men tell us, his wondrous powers persist to this day.

(1.26) Knowledgeable sources say that there was at that time a certain man who was very harsh and greedy living in Mag Inis. One day when two oxen drawing the cart of Patrick were resting and grazing in his meadow after their holy work, that foolish man drove them away by force with holy Patrick present. Holy Patrick grew angry and cursed that man saying: "Mudebroth! You have done wrong. This field will never again profit either you or your descendants forevermore. From now on it will be useless." And thus it was so. On that same day a flood from the sea came and washed over that field, as the prophet says: "a fruitful land became a marsh because of the sins of those dwelling there." Thus it has been sandy and barren from the day when holy Patrick cursed it to this present day.

Book Two

(1) Patrick's diligence in prayer
(2) How a dead man spoke to him
(3) How a Sunday night was illuminated so that horses could be found
(4) How the angel prevented him from dying in Armagh
(5) About the burning bush in which there was an angel
(6) Patrick's four requests
(7) Concerning the day of his death and his lifespan of 120 years
(8) The suspension of night and the twelve nights without darkness

(9) De sacrificio ab episcopo Tassach accepto
(10) De uigilis primae noctis iuxta corpus Patricii quas angeli fecerunt
(11) De consilio sepulturae eius ab angelo
(12) De igne de sepulcro eius erumpente
(13) De freto sussum surgente, ut non bellum de corpore fieret
(14) De felici seductione populorum

(2.1) De dilegentia orationis <eius pauca de multis quae enarrare possumus scribere conabimur>. Omnes psalmos et ymnos et Apocalipsin Iohannis et omnia kantica spiritalia scripturarum cotidie decantans siue manens aut in itenere pergens, tropeo etiam crucis in omni hora diei noctisque centies se signans et ad omnes cruces quascumque uidisset orationis gratia de curru discendens declinabat.

(2.2) Inde etiam in die quadam ingrediens crucem, quae erat iuxta uiam sita, non uidens praetergressus est. Hanc tamen auriga uidit, et ille dixit cum ad hospitum quoddam quo tenderat peruenissent et orare ante prandium coepissent, dixit, inquam, auriga: "Vidi crucem iuxta uiam per quam uenimus positam." At ille dimisso hospito per uiam quam uenerat pergens orauit, et sepulcrum ibi uiderat, et mortuum in illo busto sepultum interrogauit qua morte abierat et sub fide uixerat. Respondit mortuus: "Gentilis uixi et hic sepultus fui. Quaedam etiam mulier in alia prouincia degens mortuum filium qui se longue separatus erat habuit et illa absente sepultus est; at post aliquot dies lugens mater omissum filium planxit et indiscreto errore sepulchrum gentilis hominis sui filii bustum esse putans crucem iuxta gentilem possuit." Et ob hanc caussam, ut Patricius dixit, crucem non uiderat quia sepulturae gentilis locus fuit. Et uirtus maior inde surrexerat, ut mortuus loqueretur et qui sub fide defunctus erat Christi scieretur et iuxta illum almae crucis fieret meritum signo in uero termino possito.

(9) The sacrament given to him by bishop Tassach
(10) The vigil of the first night at Patrick's body performed by angels
(11) Advice from an angel about his tomb
(12) How fire burst forth from his tomb
(13) How the sea rose so that there would not be a battle over his body
(14) How the people were happily misled

(2.1) Concerning the diligence of his prayers, we will try to record a few of the many things we might say. Every day, whether he was in one place or traveling, Patrick would sing all the psalms and hymns and the Apocalypse of John and all the spiritual songs of the scriptures. Every hour of the day and night he would make the sign of the cross upon himself a hundred times. And whenever he saw a cross he would come down from his chariot and go before it to pray.

(2.2) One day Patrick was on a journey when he passed by a cross on the side of the road. He did not see it, but his charioteer did. When they came to a certain guest house which had been their destination they began to pray before eating. The driver then said: "I saw a cross on the side of the road which we passed." Patrick left the guest house and went back along the road they had followed and prayed. There he saw the grave. He then asked the dead man buried there how he had died and whether he had lived in the Christian faith. The dead man said: "I was a pagan and here I was buried. There was a woman from another province whose son had died here far from her. She was absent when he was buried, but some time later she came here mourning and lamenting her lost son. She was so upset that she mistook my grave for his, thinking a pagan's tomb belonged to her son and thus placed the cross here." Patrick therefore said that since it was the grave of a pagan, he had not seen the cross. But Patrick's great power is shown, however, because he caused a dead man to speak. The man who had died in the faith was made known and the nourishing cross was moved to its rightful place beside his grave.

(2.3) Consuitudo autem illi erat ut a uespera dominicae noctis usque ad mane secundae feriae Patricius non ambularet inde. In quadam dominica die honre sacri temporis in campo pernoctans grauis pluia cum tempestate accederat, sed cum grauis pluia in tota patria populata est in loco ubi sanctus episcopus pernoctabat siccitas erat sicut in conca et in uellere Gedeon accederat. Auriga, memorat equos amissos, quasi amicos caros planguit, quia illos quaerere tenebris arcentibus uissum non poterat. Inde pietas Patricii patris pii mota est et flebili aurigae dixit: "Deus in angustis inoportunitatibus adiutor prumptus adiutorium praestabit et equos quos ploras inuenies." Exhinc manum spolians manica extensam eleuauit et quinque digiti sicut luminaria ita proxima quaeque inluxerant et per lucem extensae manus equos quos amisserat auriga solutu gemitu inuenit. Sed hoc miraculum auriga comes usque ad Patricii obitum absconderat.

(2.4) Post uero miracula tanta, quae alibi scripta sunt et quae ore fideli mundus celebrat adpropinquante die mortis eius uenit ad eum angelus et dixit illi de morte sua. Ideo ad Ardd Machae missit, quam prae omnibus terris dilexit; ideo mandauit ut uenirent ad eum uiri multi ad eundem deducendum quo uoluit. Inde cum comittibus suis iter carpere coepit ad Machi uoluntariae, tellurem cupitam satis.

(2.5) Sed iuxta uiam rubus quaedam arserat et non conburebatur sicut antea Moysi prouenerat. In rubo Victor erat anguelus, qui Patricium sepe uissitare solebat, et Victor alterum anguelum ad Patricium prohibendum ne pergat quo pergere cupit missit, et dixit illi: "Quare proficisceris sine Victoris consilio? Quam ob rem Victor te uocat, et ad eum declina." Et ut ei iussum est declinauit et quid facere deberet interrogauit. Et respondens anguelus dixerat: "Reuertere ad locum unde uenis, hoc est Sabul, et datae sunt quattuor petitiones tibi quas petisti."

(2.3) It was the habit of Patrick not to travel from the evening of the Lord's night until the morning of the second day of the week. One Sunday when he was spending the night in a field in honor of this sacred time, a great rain storm began. But although the whole land was soaked with heavy rain, the spot where the holy bishop stayed remained dry just as in the story of Gideon's bowl and fleece. Patrick's charioteer realized the horses had wandered away and wept for them as for dear friends, unable as he was to search for them on account of the dark. Dear father Patrick was moved by kindness and said to the weeping charioteer: "God always hears us in our great misfortunes and will help us now. You will find the horses you are crying about." Then he rolled up his sleeve, drew out his hand, and raised his five fingers in the air so that they flooded the area with light. The charioteer found his lost horses and ceased his weeping. But the charioteer did not reveal this miracle until after Patrick's death.

(2.4) After so many miracles which the world celebrates, some written down and others passed on piously by word of mouth, the day of his death was approaching and an angel came to speak with him about it. Thus Patrick sent word to Armagh, because he loved that place above all the lands on earth. He ordered that many men might come and bring him to the place he much desired. Then with his companions he began his journey to his beloved Armagh, the land of his longing.

(2.5) But next to the road there was a certain bush burning but not consumed, just as it was with Moses. In the bush was the angel Victor who used to visit Patrick often. Victor sent another angel to stop him from going where he wished to go, and the angel said to him: "Why do you journey without consulting Victor? He is calling you now, so turn aside to see him." As he was ordered, Patrick turned aside and asked Victor what he ought to do. And the angel said: "Return to the place from which you came (i.e. to Saul)[31] and the four petitions which you sought will be granted to you."

31. *Saul*: Near Downpatrick, County Down.

(2.6) "Prima petetio, ut in Ardd Machae fiat ordinatio tua. Secunda petitio, ut quicumque ymnum qui de te conpossitus est in die exitus de corpore cantauerit, tu iudicabis poenitentiam eius de suis peccatis. Tertia petitio, ut nepotes Dichon, qui te benigne susciperunt, missericordiam mereantur et non pereant. Quarta petitio, ut Hibernenses omnes in die iudicii a te iudicentur—sicut dicitur ad apostolos: *Et uos sedentes iudicabitis duodecim tribus Israel*[s]—ut eos quibus apostolus fuisti iudices."

(2.7) "Reuertere igitur sicut tibi dico, et moriens ingredieris uiam patrum tuorum." Quod in die xui. kalendas Aprilis peractis totius eius uitae annis centum uiginti ei prouenerat sicut omnibus totius Hyberniae annis celebratur.

(2.8) "Et contra noctem terminum pones," quia in illa die mortis eius nox non erat et per duodecim dies in illa prouincia in qua mortis eius exequiae peractae sunt nox non inruit et fuscis tellurem non amplexerat alis et pallor non tantus erat noctis et astriferas non induxerat Bosferas umbras; et plebs Ulod dixit quod usque in finem anni totius in quo abierat numquam noctium tales tenebrae erant quales antea fuerunt, quod ad tanti uiri meritum declarandum esse dubium est. Si quis autem terminum contra noctem et noctem non uissam esse in tota prouincia breui tempore in quo luctus Patricii peractus est abnegare infideliter uoluit, audiat et diligenter attendat qualiter Ezechiae languenti in horalogio Acaz demonstrato sanitatis indicio sol per decem lineas recurrens ostensus sit paene duplicato die et sicut *sol contra Gabaon et luna contra uallem Achilon stetit.*[t]

(2.9) Adpropinquante autem hora obitus sui sacrificium ab episcopo Tassach, sicut illi Victor anguelus dixit, ad uiaticum beatae uitae acciperat.

(2.10) In prima nocte exequiarum eius angueli uigilias almi corporis fecerunt in uigiliarum et psalmorum moribus, omnibus

s. Mt 19.28 t. Jos 10.12

(2.6) "The first petition is that your rule might be in Armagh. The second petition is that whoever sings the hymn composed by you on the day of his death will have his penance for sins determined by you. The third petition is that the descendants of Díchu, who welcomed you so kindly, shall deserve mercy and not perish. The fourth petition is that all the Irish will be judged by you on the day of judgment—just as it was said to the apostles: 'And you shall sit judging the twelve tribes of Israel'—so that you as their apostle might judge them."

(2.7) "Return therefore as I have said to you, and when you die you will enter the way of your fathers." And thus it happened on the seventeenth of March—with the years of his life numbering one hundred and twenty—and all of Ireland celebrates this day every year.

(2.8) "And you will set a barrier against the night." And on the day of Patrick's death there was no night for twelve days throughout the province as they celebrated his passing. Night did not rush down or embrace the earth with its dark wings. Neither was there the dusk of night nor did evening bring in star-bearing shadows. The tribe of the Ulaid say that until the end of the year in which he died the nights were not as dark as they had been before. Surely this was to declare the merits of such a great man. If anyone doubts that night was suspended and throughout the whole province darkness was not seen during the brief time Patrick was mourned, let him listen and carefully pay attention to the story of Hezekiah. As a sign of his healing, he saw the sun going backwards over ten lines of the sundial of Ahaz so that the day was almost doubled in length. Note also how "the sun stood still at Gibeon and the moon in the valley of Aijalon."

(2.9) With the hour of his death approaching, Patrick received the sacrament from bishop Tassach as food for his journey to the blessed life, just as the angel Victor had told him.

(2.10) During the first night after his death, angels kept a vigil over his dear body with prayers and psalms, for all the men who had

quicumque ad uigilias in illa prima nocte ueniebant dormientibus. In ceteris autem noctibus homines orantes et psalmos cantantes corpus custodierunt. Postquam autem in caelum profecti sunt angueli odorem suauissimum quasi mellis et flagrantiam dulcidinis quasi uini dimisserunt, ut impleretur quod in benedictionibus patriarchae Iacob dictum est: *Ecce odor filii mei tamquam odor agri pleni quem benedixit Dominus.*[u]

(2.11) Quando autem anguelus ad eum uenit consilium sepulturae dedit illi: "Elegantur duo boues indomiti et pergant quocumque uoluerint, et ubicumque requiescunt aeclessia in honorem corpusculi tui aedificetur." Et sicut anguelus dixit instabiles electi sunt iuuenci et stabili plaustrum gestamine humeris inpossitum cum sancto corpore uechunt, et a loco qui Clocher uocatur ab oriente Findubrec de pecoribus Conail electo clarificauit boues, et exierunt nutu Dei regente ad Dun Lethglaisse, ubi sepultus est Patricius.

(2.12) Et dixit ei: "Ne reliquiae a terra reducantur corporis tui, et cubitus de terra super corpus fiat." Quod iussu Dei factum in nouissimis demonstratum est temporibus, quia quando aeclessia super corpus facta est fodientes humum antropi ignem a sepulchro erumpere uiderunt et recedentes flammigerum timuerunt flammae ignem.

(2.13) De reliquiis sancti Patricii in tempore obitus sui dira contensio ad bellum usque perueniens inter neoptes Neill et orientales ex una parte, inter aliquando propinquales et propinquos, nunc inter dirissimos hostes, irarum intrat certamen. Sed fretum quoddam quod Collum Bouis uocatur merito Patricii, ne sanguis effunderetur, et misercordia Dei, altis crispantibusque intumescebat fluctibus et undarum uertices concaua rumpebant aera et dorsa in fluctibus tremula crispanti rissu et aliquando flauis uallibus in certamine ruebant; quasi ad cohibendam animossitatem gentium dirarum—tales enim populi sunt—surrexit freti feritas et plebes pugnare prohibuit.

u. Gn 27.27

come to keep vigil fell asleep. In the other nights men prayed and sang psalms while they watched over the body. But after the angels had returned to heaven they left behind a sweet smell like honey or the fragrance that comes from wine. This fulfilled the blessing of the patriarch Jacob who said: "Behold, the smell of my son is like a fruitful field blessed by the Lord."

(2.11) When an angel came to Patrick he gave him advice concerning his tomb: "Let two unbroken oxen be chosen and let them wander wherever they wish. Wherever they stop, build a church there in honor of your remains." As the angel said, the untamed oxen were chosen and with a harness around there necks pulled the cart containing the holy body. And from the place called Clocher to the east of Findabair the place was chosen by the oxen of Conal. Ruled by the will of God, they went to Dún Lethglaisse,[32] where the tomb of Patrick is.

(2.12) And the angel said to Patrick: "So that your body will not be removed from the ground, let it be covered by a cubit of earth." That this order came from God is shown by recent events. When a church was being built there over the body, the men who were digging saw fire shoot up from the tomb. They immediately fled in terror of the flame.

(2.13) At the time of Patrick's death a struggle over his relics arose that was so great it led to war between the Uí Néill[33] and their eastern allies against the Ulaid. Once they were friendly neighbors, but now they are bitter enemies. But to prevent bloodshed, the inlet of the sea called Druimm Bó arose by the merits of Patrick and the mercy of God. It rose up high in swirling waves with their crests bursting through the air as in a race to quench the rage of these warring tribes—for that is the sort of people they are. Thus the rising of the raging sea stopped the tribes from fighting.

32. *Dún Lethglaisse*: Downpatrick, County Down.

33. The *Uí Néill* were a confederation of tribes which spread east from Connaught in the early Christian period at the expense of the Ulaid tribes of Ulster and the tribes of northern Leinster.

(2.14) Postea autem sepulto Patricio et freti tumore sedato orientales et nepotes Neill contra Ultu acriter ad certamen ruunt et certatim praeparati et armati ad bellum ad locum beati corporis prorumperat, sed felici seducti sunt fallacia putantes se duos boues et plaustrum inuenire et corpus sanctum rapere aestimabant et cum corpore et tali praeparatu et armatura usque ad fluium Cabcenne peruenierunt et corpus tunc illis non conparuit. Inpossibile enim ut de tanto ac de beato corpore pax fieret nissi Dei nutu taliter uideretur uissio ad tempus ostensa, ne quod animarum salus innumerabilium in exitum et mortem uerteretur; sicut Siri antea excaecati, ne sanctum profetam Helesseum occiderent, ad Helesseum diuina prouissione ad Samariam usque ducti sunt, haec etiam seductio ad concordiam populorum facta est.

(2.14) After Patrick was buried and the sea had calmed, the easterners and the Uí Néill again rushed to battle the Ulaid. Ready and armed for war they invaded the resting place of the holy body. But they were fortunately misled by an illusion. They thought they saw two oxen pulling the cart and believed they were seizing the holy body. With the body and all their weapons they came as far as the Cabcenne river—but then the body vanished from their sight. For it was impossible that there would be peace concerning such a famous and blessed body unless God had showed them such a vision at that time. If not, the salvation of countless souls would have been turned to destruction and death. In the same way in ancient times, the Syrians were blinded so that they could not kill the prophet Elisha.[34] By divine providence they were led by Elisha as far as Samaria. Thus this illusion brought peace to the people.

34. V. 2Kgs 6.11–20.

TIRECHANI COLLECTANEA DE SANCTO PATRICIO

Tirechan episcopus haec scripsit ex ore uel libro Ultani episcopi, cuius ipse alumpnus uel discipulus fuit.

(1) Inueni .iiii. nomina in libro scripta Patricio apud Ultanum episcopum Conchuburnensium: sanctus Magonus, qui est clarus; Succetus, qui est ***; Patricius <***>; Cothirthiacus, quia seruiuit .iiii. domibus magorum; et empsit illum unus ex eis, cui nomen erat Miliuc maccu Boin magus, et seruiuit illi .uii. annis omni seruitute ac duplici labore, et porcarium possuit eum in montanis conuallibus. Deinde autem uissitauit illum anguelus Domini in somniis in cacuminibus montis Scirte iuxta montem Miss. Finita autem angueli sentenia "Ecce nauis tua parata: surge et ambula," et secessit ab illo in caelum, surrexit et ambulauit, et ut dixit illi anguelus Domini Victor nomine. In septimo decimo aetatis suae anno captus ductus, uenditus est in Hiberniam, In uicesimo secundo anno laboris magis relinquere potuit. Septem aliis annis ambulauit et nauigauit in fluctibus et in campistribus locis et in conuallibus montanis per Gallias atque Italiam totam atque in insolis quae sunt in mare Terreno, ut ipse dixit in commemoratione laborum. Erat autem in una ex insolis, quae dicitur Aralanensis, annis triginta mihi testante Ultano episcopo. Omnia autem quae euenierunt inuenietis in plana illius historia scripta. Haec sunt nouissima illius mirabilia in quinto regni anno Loiguiri Maicc Neill finita atque feliciter facta.

1.5 *Bie.*[3]: *Succetus, qui est <deus belli; Patricius, qui est> pater ciuium.*

TÍRECHÁN'S *JOURNEY OF ST. PATRICK*

The Collection of Tírechán concerning Saint Patrick

Bishop Tírechán wrote these things taken from the words and book of Bishop Ultán,[1] whose foster child and pupil he was.

(1) I have found four names[2] for Patrick written in a book by Ultán, bishop of Conchubair: holy *Magonus*, that is "famous"; *Succetus*, that is ***; Patricius <***>; *Cothirtiacus*, because he served four houses of druids. And one of these, named Miliuc maccu Bóin, bought him. Patrick served him for seven years in every kind of servitude and heavy labor. Miliuc made him a swineherd in the mountain valleys. Finally however an angel of the Lord visited him in his sleep on the top of Sliab Scirit near Sliab Miss.[3] When an angel had finished telling him, "Behold, your ship is ready.[4] Get up and walk" and had gone back into the sky, Patrick got up and walked. The name of that angel was Victor. In his seventeenth year, Patrick was taken into slavery and sold in Ireland. In his twenty-second year he was able to leave the service of the druid. For seven other years he walked and sailed by sea and in plains and mountain valleys through Gaul and all of Italy and among islands in the Tyrrhenian Sea, as he said himself in describing his work. He was on one of these islands, which is called Aralensis,[5] for thirty years as Bishop Ultán told me. However you will find all that happened to him written in the plain account of his life. These are the latest of his miracles happily completed in the fifth year of the reign of Loíguire son of Niall.[6]

1. Ultán was bishop of Árdbraccan in Dál Conchubair, Meath, and died in 657.
2. Cf. Muirchú Prologue, 1.1.
3. *Slíab Miss*: Slemish, County Antrim.
4. The man Victoricus of Patrick's *Conf.* 23 has become the angel Victor.
5. *Aralanensis*: Possibly Lérins, near the coast west of Marseilles (cf. *Sayings of Patrick* 1).
6. Loíguire, son of Níall, was high king of Ireland at Tara in Meath (cf. Muirchú *Life* 1.10ff.).

(2) A passione autem Christi colleguntur anni quadringenti triginta tres usque ad mortem Patricii. Duobus autem uel quinque annis regnauit Loiguire post mortem Patricii. Omnis autem regni illius tempus triginta sex, ut putamus.

(3) Venit uero Patricius cum Gallis ad insolas Maccu Chor et insola orientali, quae dicitur Insola Patricii, et secum fuit multitudo episcoporum sanctorum et praespiterorum et diaconorum ac exorcistarum, hostiariorum lectoremque nec non filiorum quos ordinauit.

(4) Ascendit autem de mari ad campum Breg sole orto cum benedictione Dei, cum uero sole mirae doctrinae, densas tenebras ignorantiae inluminans. Ad Hiberniam ingens lucifer sanctus episcopus oritur, et antifana assiduo erat ei de fine ad finem "In nomine Domini Dei Patris et Filii atque Spiritus Sancti." +Iesu Christi benigni+ Hoc autem dicitur in Scotia lingua *Ochen.*

(5) Primo uero uenit ad uallem Sescnani et aedificauit ibi aeclessiam primam et portauit filium Sesceneum nomine episcopum secum et reliuit ibi .ii. pueros perigrinos. Vespere uero uenit ad hostium Albine ad quendam uirum bonum et babtitzauit illum, et uenit cum illo filium placitum sibi et dedit illi nomen Benignum, quia collegebat pedes Patricii inter manus suas et pectus et noluit dormire apud patrem et matrem, sed fleuit nissi cum Patricio dormiret. Mane autem facto cum surgerent, conpleta benedictione super patrem Benigni Patricius currum conscendit et pedes illius diuerso alter in curru et alter super terram erat, et Benignus puer pedem Patricii tenuit duabus manibus strictis et clamauit: "Sinite me apud Patricium patrem proprium mihi," et dixit Patricius: "Babtitzate eum et eleuate eum in currum, quia heres regni mei est." Ipse est Benignus episcopus, successor Patricii in aeclesia Machae.

(2) From the passion of Christ to the death of Patrick are reckoned 433 years. However Loíguire ruled for two or five years after Patrick's death. The length of his reign was thirty-six years, as we calculate.

(3) Patrick came with his Gauls to the islands of Moccu Chor and to the eastern island known as the island of Patrick.[7] With him were many holy bishops, priests, deacons, exorcists, porters, and lectors, as well as a number of sons he ordained.

(4) He went up from the sea to Mag Breg[8] at sunrise with the blessing of God, with the true sun of wondrous doctrine, illuminating the darks shadows of ignorance. The great light-bearing holy bishop rose over Ireland and his song from beginning to end was: "In the name of the Father, the Lord God, et the Son and the Holy Spirit." In the Irish language this is called the *Ochen*.

(5) First he came to the valley of Sescnán and built there his first church and left behind there two foreign boys. In the evening he came to the mouth of the Ailbhine river to a certain good man and baptized him. He found with him a son who pleased him and gave him the name Benignus[9] because the boy held Patrick's feet between his hands and chest, not wishing to sleep with his father and mother but cried unless he was allowed to sleep with Patrick. In the morning however when they arose and Patrick had blessed the father of Benignus and had gone up into his chariot, Benignus held the feet of Patrick in his hands tightly and cried out: "Allow me to be with Patrick, my true father." And Patrick said: "Baptize him and lift him onto my chariot, for he is the heir to my kingdom." This one is Bishop Benignus, the successor of Patrick at the church of Armagh.

7. V. Muirchú 1.11.

8. *Mag* (Irish "plain") is a translation for Latin *campum*. *Mag Breg* is in County Meath.

9. Cf. Muirchú 1.20.

(6) De episcoporum numero quos ordinauit in Hibernia quadringentos quinquaginta. De praespiteris non possimus ordinare, quia babtizabat cotidie homines et illis litteras legebat ac abgatorias <scribebat>, et de aliis episcopus ac praespiteros faciebat, qui in aetate babtismum acciperunt sobria.

(8) De aeclessiis quas fundauit in campo Breg. Primum in Culmine .ii. aeclesia Cerne, in qua sepultus est Hercus, qui portauit mortalitatem magnam .iii. in cacuminibus Aisse .iiii. i mBlaitniu .u. in Collumbus, in qua ordinauit Eugenium sanctum episcopum .ui. aeclessia filio Laithphi .uii. i mBridam in qua fuit sanctus Dulcis, frater Carthaci .uiii. super Argetbor, in qua <fuit> Kannanus episcopus, quem ordinauit Patricius in primo pasca hi ferti uirorum Feicc, qui portauit secum ignem primum benedictum ac ceriales lucernas primas Patricii de manibus portauit domini, ut accenderet fumum benedictum in oculos ac nares hominum gentilium et regis Loiguiri et magorum illius, quia contraiuerunt illi tres magi fratres ex uno uiro nominibus +et genere+ Cruth, Loch, <et> Lethlanu, de genere Runtir, qui fecerunt conflictionem magnum contra Patricium et Benignum. Cassula autem magi inflammata est circa Benignum et in cinerem finita erat. Sanctus quoque filius sanus effectus est firma fide Dei in conspectu regis et hominum et magorum, cassula autem Benigni filii Patricii infixa est circa magum et inflammatus est magus in medio ac consumptus est, et dixit Patricius: "In hac hora consumpta est gentilitas Hiberniae tota." Et eleuauit Patricius manus suas Deo circa magum +Lochletheneum+ et dixit: "Domine mi, iece a me canem qui oblatrat faciem tuam et me; eat in mortem." Et intenderunt omnes magum eleuatum per tenebras nocturnales poene usque ad caelum, sed reuersus cadauer illius congluttinatum grandinibus et niuibus, commixtum scintillis igneis in terram ante faciem

(6) Concerning the number of bishops he ordained in Ireland, there were 450. Concerning priests, we cannot give a number, because he baptized people every day and read letters to them and wrote out alphabets for them. Some of them he made bishops and priests of those who had been baptized at a sober age.[10]

(8) Concerning the churches which Patrick founded in Mag Breg. First, on the hilltop. Second, the church at Cerne where Ercc is buried. Third, on the hills of Aisse. Fourth, in Blaitine. Fifth, at Collumcille, at which Eugenius was ordained a holy bishop. Sixth, a church for the son of Lathphe. Seventh, in Bridam, where holy Dulcis lived, brother of Carthacus. Eighth, on Argetbor, where Kannanus was bishop, whom Patrick ordained on his first Easter at the burial ground of Fíacc's men, who carried with him the first holy fire and the first lighted candles from the hands of the lord Patrick. This was to bear the blessed smoke into the eyes and nose of the pagan men and King Loíguire and his druids. For three druids opposed Patrick: Cruth, Loch, and Lethanu, brothers of one man, from the tribe of Runtir. These men started a great confrontation with Patrick and Benignus. The cloak of the druid was burned and became ashes around Benignus. The holy boy was saved by his firm faith in God in the sight of the king and his men and the druids. But the cloak of Benignus the son of Patrick was worn by the druid who was burned to death in it before in the middle of them. And Patrick said: "In this hour all the paganism of Ireland has been burnt away." And Patrick raised his hands to God because of the druid Lochletheneus and said: "My Lord, cast away from me this dog who barks at your face and at me.[11] Let him go to his death." And everyone watched the druid lifted up through the dark night almost to the sky. But coming back down, his corpse was covered with hail and snow mixed with sparks of fire and fell down before them all. The druid's stone on

10. At this point the *Book of Armagh* inserts a list (omitted here) of over seventy churchmen which was probably not originally in Tírechán manuscript.

11. Compare the similar canine insults Jerome makes against Pelagius (*Commentary on Jeremiah* 3).

omnium cecidit; et est lapsis illius in oris australibus orientalibusque <Temro> usque in praesentem diem, et conspexi illum oculis meis.

(9) Prima feria uenit ad Taltenam, ubi fit agon regale, ad Coirpriticum filium Neill, qui uoluit eum occidere et flagillauit seruos eius in flumine Séle, ut indicarent Patricium Coirpritico; quapropter appellabat illum Patricius inimicum Dei et dixit ei: "Semen tuum seruiet seminibus fratrum et non erit de semine tuo rex in aeternum; et non erunt pisces magni in flumine Séle semper."

(10) Deinde autem uenit ad Conallum filium Neill ad domum illius, quam fundauit in loco in quo est hodie Aeclessia Patricii Magna, et suscepit eum cum gaudio magno et babtitzauit illum et firmauit solium eius in aeternum et dixit illi: "Semen fratrum tuorum tuo semini seruiet in aeternum. Et tu missericordiam debes facere heredibus meis post me in saeculum et filii tui et filiorum tuorum filiis meis credulis legitimum sempiternum." Pensabatque aeclessiam Deo Patricii pedibus eius sexaginta pedum, et dixit Patricius: "Si dimimuatur aeclessia ista, non erit longum regnum tibi et firmum."

(11) Pasca quoque claussa finita prima feria exiit ad Vadum Molae et ibi aeclessiam fundauit, in qua reliquit tres fratres cum una sorore, et haec sunt nomina illorum: Cathaceus, Cathurus, Catneus, et soror illorum Catnea, quae emulgebat lac ab dammulis feris, ut senes mihi indicauerunt.

(12) Perrexitque ad ciuitatem Temro ad Logairium filium Neill iterum, quia apd illum foedus pepigit, ut non occideretur in regno illius; sed non potuit credere, dicens: "Nam Neel pater meus non siniuit mihi credere, sed ut sepeliar in cacuminibus Temro quasi uiris consistentibus in bello" (quia utuntur gentiles in sepulcris armati prumptis armis) "facie ad faciem usque ad diem *erdathe*"

which he fell is in the southeastern part of Tara to this present day and I have seen it with my own eyes.

(9) On the first day Patrick came to Coirpritius, son of Niall, at Tailtiu[12] where there was a royal assembly. Coirpritius wished to kill him and so had his servants whipped in the Séle river[13] to make them point out Patrick to him. Because of this Patrick called him the enemy of God and said to him: "Your seed will serve the seed of your brothers and there will never again be a king from your descendents. There will also no longer be large fish in the Séle river."

(10) Then he came to Conall son of Niall in his house which he had built which is now the Great Church of Patrick.[14] Conall received him with great joy and Patrick baptized him and established his throne forever, saying to him: "The seed of your brothers will serve your seed forever. You must give alms to my heirs after me always. Your sons and the sons of your sons must pay tribute to my sons forever." And he measured out a church for the God of Patrick sixty feet long with his own feet. And Patrick said: "If anything is taken from this church, your reign will be neither long nor secure."

(11) At the end of Easter, when Sunday was over, he went out to the Ford of the Mill and there founded a church, in which he left three brothers and one sister. These are their names: Cathaceus, Cathurus, Catneus, and their sister Catnea, who milked wild deer, as old people have told me.

(12) And he again to the city of Tara[15] to Loíguire son of Niall, because he had made an agreement with him that he would not be killed on his lands. But Loíguire was not able to believe, saying: "My father Niall would not allow me to accept your religion, but I am to be buried in the mounds of Tara as if facing men in war" (for the pagans are buried in their graves armed) "face to face until the day

12. *Tailtiu*: Teltown near Kells in County Meath.
13. *Séle*: the Blackwater river.
14. *Great Church*: Donaghpatrick in County Meath.
15. *Tara*: traditional seat of the high kings of Ireland in County Meath.

(apud magos, id est iudicii diem Domini) "ego filius Neill et filius Dúnlinge imMaistin in campo Liphi pro duritate odii ut est hoc."

(13) Porro fundauit aeclessiam i Carric Dagri et alteram aeclessiam i mMruig Thuaithe, et scripsit elimenta Cerpano; et intrauit in domum regiam et non surrexerunt ante se nissi unus tantum, hoc est Hercus sacrilegus, et dixit illi: "Cur tu solus surrexisti in honorem Dei mei in me?" Et dixit ei Hercus: "Nescio quid, uideo scintellas igneas de labiis tuis ascendere in labia mea." Sanctus quoque dixit: "Si babtisma Domini accipies, quod mecum est?" Respondit: "Accipiam," et uenierunt ad fontem Loigles in Scotica, nobiscum "Vitulus Ciuitatum." Cumque aperuisset librum atque babtitzasset uirum Hercum, audiuit uiros post tergum suum se inridentes ad inuicem de rei illius consideratione, quia nescierunt quid fecerat; et babtitzauit tot milia hominum in die illa.

(14) Et inter caeteras babtismatis sententias <***> audiuit. Ecce .ii. namque uiri nobiles confabulabantur post tergum sibi, et dixit alter alteri: "Verum est quod dixisti a circulo anni qui praeteriit, ut ueniisses huc in illis diebus? Dic mihi nomen tuum, quaesso, et patris tui et agri tui et campi tui et ubi est domus tua." Respondit: "Endeus filius Amolngid sum ego, filii Fechrach filii Echach, ab occidentalibus plagis de campo Domnon et silua Fochloth." Cumque audiisset Patricius nomen siuae Fochlothi, gauissus est ualde et dixit Endeo Amolngid filio: "Et ego tecum exibo, si uiuus fuero, quia dixit mihi Dominus exire," et dixit Endeus: "Non exibis mecum, ne occidamur ad iuuicem." Sanctus quoque dixit: "Verumtamen numquam uiuus ad tuam regionem peruenies et tu, nissi uenero tecum, et uitam aeternam non habebis,

of *erdathe*"[16] (among the druids this is the day of the Lord's judgment). "I the son of Niall facing the son of Dúnlaing in Maistiu[17] in Mag Liphe because of the fierceness of our hatred it is thus."

(13) He also founded a church at Carrac Dagri and another at Mruig Túaithe, and he wrote an alphabet for Cerpanus. And he entered the king's palace and they did not rise before him except one only, this was Erc, a pagan. And he said to Erc: "Why do you alone rise in honor of my God?" And Erc said to him: "I don't know what it is. I see fiery sparks rising from your lips to mine." The holy man also spoke saying: "Will you receive the baptism of the Lord which I bring?" He responded: "I accept." And they went to the well called Loígles[18] in Irish, but with us "Calf of the Cities." And when he opened the book and baptized the man Erc, he heard men behind him laughing among themselves at him because of his action, for they did not understand what he had done. And he baptized many thousands of people on that day.

(14) And while he was finishing the baptismal formula he heard <***>. Behold two men were talking to each other behind him and one said to the other: "Is it true that this time last year you said you would come here in these days? Please tell me your name and your father's name and your land and territory and where your home is." The other replied: "I am Énde son of Amolngid son of Fiachrae son of Echu from the western part of Mag Domnon and the wood of Fochloth."[19] When Patrick heard the name of the wood of Fochloth he was very happy and said to Énde son of Amolngid: "I will go with you, if I am still alive, for the Lord told me to go with you." And Énde said to him: "You will not go with me for we both may be killed." And the holy man replied: "Quite the opposite, for you will not reach your lands again unless I come with you and you will

16. If the day of *erdathe* (Irish, perhaps "fate, unhappy ending") is a genuine druidic belief, this is one of the few surviving references to Irish pagan eschatology.

17. *Maistiu*: Mullaghmast, County Kildare.

18. *Loígles*: Irish *loíg* ("calf"), *les* ("pen, enclosure"), probably on the hill of Tara.

19. *wood of Fochloth*: On the western shore of Killala Bay, County Mayo. In Patrick's *Confession* (23), it is the place from which he receives his call to return to the Irish.

quia propter me uenisti huc quasi Ioseph ante filios Israel. Endeus autem dixit Patricio: "Tu filio meo babtismum da, quia tener est; ego autem et fratres mei non possimus tibi credere usque dum ad nostram plebem peruenerimus, ne inrideant nos." Conallus autem babtitzatus est, et dedit Patricius benedictionem super illum et tenuit manum illius et dedit Cethiacho episcopo, et nutriuit illum et docuit eum Cethiachus et Mucneus frater Cethiachi episcopi, cuius sunt reliquiae in aeclessia magna Patricii in silua Fochlithi. Propter hoc mandauit Conallo insolam suam Cethiachus, et generis illius est usque in praesentem diem, quia laicus fuit post mortem Cethichi sancti.

(15) Venierunt autem filii Amolngid sex ad iudicandum ante faciem Loiguiri, et Endeus contra eos unus et filius eius tener et Patricius ante illos, et inuestigaucrunt causam hereditatis illorum, et iudicauit illis Loiguire et Patricius, ut diuiderent inter se hereditatem in septem partes. Et dixit Endeus: "Filium meum et partem hereditatis meae ego immolo Deo Patricii et Patricio." Per hoc dicunt alii quia serui sumus Patricii usque in praesentem diem. Foedus pepigerunt per manus Loiguiri filii Neill Patricius et filii Amolngid cum exercitu laicorum <et> episcoporum sanctorum et inierunt iter facere ad montem Egli, et extendit Patricius etiam praetium quindecim animarum hominum, ut in scriptione sua adfirmat, de argento et auro, ut nullus malorum hominum inpederet eos in uia recta transeuntes totam Hiberniam, quia necessitas poscit illos ut peruenirent siluam Fochliti ante caput anni pasca secunda causa filiorum clamantium clamore magno, <quorum> uoces audiuit in utero matrum suarum dicentium: "Veni, sancte Patrici, saluos nos facere."

(16) Plantauit aeclessiam super Vadum Segi et alteram aeclessiam Cinnene sanctae super Vadum Carnoi i mBoind et altera super Coirp raithe et altera super fossam Dallbronig, quam tenuit episcopus filius Cairtin, auunculus Brigtae sanctae. Funauit

not have eternal life. For it is because of me you came here, just as Joseph came before the sons of Israel." But Énde said to Patrick: "Baptize my son, for he is young. However, I and my brothers are not able to believe in you until we come to our people lest they laugh at us." Conall was therefore baptized, and Patrick blessed him and held his hand and gave him over to Bishop Cethiachus. And Cethiachus brought him up and taught him, as did Mucneus, brother of Bishop Cethiachus, whose relics are in the great church of Patrick in the wood of Fochloth. Because of this Cethiachus entrusted his monastery to Conall, whose family owns it to the present day, because he was still a layman after holy Cethiachus died.

(15) The six sons of Amolngid came into the presence of Loíguire for judgment. And Énde alone stood against them and his young son and Patrick. And they investigated the claims of their inheritance and Loíguire and Patrick judged them that they should divide their inheritance between them in seven parts. And Énde said: "My son and my share of the inheritance I offer to the God of Patrick and to Patrick." For this reason, some say, we are servants of Patrick to the present day.[20] Patrick and the sons of Amolngid along with the lay assembly and the holy bishops reached an agreement under the guarantee of Loíguire son of Níall that they should travel to Slieb Aigle. And Patrick also paid the price of fifteen men, as he says in his writings, in gold and silver, so that no man should impede them as they travelled straight across as they crossed all of Ireland. It was necessary they should arrive at the wood of Fochloth before the end of the year, that is by the next Easter, because he had heard a great call of children crying out from the wombs of their mothers whose voices were saying: "Come, holy Patrick, save us!"

(16) Patrick founded a church at Áth Segi, and another for holy Cinnena at Áth Carnoi on the Boyne. He founded another above Coirp Raithe, and another on the rath of Dallbrónach which Bishop Cairthin held, an uncle of holy Brigid.[21] He established another

20. Tírechán was a descendant of Énde.
21. St. Brigid founded a famous monastery at Kildare.

alteram in campo Echredd, alteram in campo Taidcni, quae dicitur Cell Bile (apud familiam Scire est), alteram in campo Echnach, in qua fuit Cassanus praespiter, alteram in Singitibus, alteram in campo Bili iuxta Vadum Capitis Canis, alteram in Capite Carmelli in campo Teloch, in qua sancta Brigita pallium cepit sub manibus filii Caille in Huisniuch Midi. Mansit iuxta Petram Coithrigi, sed occissi sunt circa se alii perigrini a filio Fechach filii Neill; cui maledixit dicens: "Non erit de stirpe tua rex, sed seruies semini fratrum tuorum." Et alteram aeclessiam in Capite Airt in regionibus Roide, in qua possuit altare lapideum, et alteram hi Cuil Corrae. Et uenit per flumen Ethne in duas Tethbias et ordinauit Melum episcopum, et aeclessiam Bili fundauit et ordinauit Gosactum filium Milcon maccu Booin, quem nutriuit in seruitute septem annorum, et mittens Camulacum Commiensium in campum Cumi et digito illi indicauit locum de cacumine Graneret, id est aeclessiam Raithin. Et uenit in campum Rein et ordinauit Bruscum praespiterum et aeclessiam illi fundauit; qui dixit mirabile post mortem eius altero sancto, qui fuit in insola generis Cotirbi: "Bene est tibi dum filium tuum habes; ego autem, tedebit me mors mea, quia solus sum in aeclessia in diserto, in aeclessia relicta ac uacua, et non offerent iuxta me sacerdotes." In noctibus <tribus> somnium factus est: tertio die surrexit sanctus et arripuit anulum et trullam ferrumque et sepulcri fossam fodiuit et portauit ossa Brusci sancti secum ad insolam in qua sunt, et resticuit.

(17) Mittens autem Patricius Nieth Brain ad fossam Slecht, barbarum Patricii propinquum, qui dicebat mirablia in Deo uera. Venitque Patricius ad aleum Sinone ad locum in quo mortuus fuit auriga illius Boidmalus et sepultus ibi in quo dicitur Caill Boidmail usque in hunc diem et immolatum erat Patricio. Finit liber

church at Mag Echredd, another at Mag Taidcni, which is called Cell Bile (it now belongs to the community of Scíre), another at Mag Echnach, where Cassanus was priest. He founded a church at Singite, another at Mag Bili next to the Ford of the Dog Head, another at Carmell's head at Mag Teloch, where holy Brigid received the veil from the hands of Mac Caille in Uisnech in Mide. He stayed near Coithrige's Rock, but some of his foreign companions were killed by the son of Fíachu son of Níall. Patrick cursed him saying: "None of your descendants will be king, but you will serve the seed of your brothers." He founded another church at Art's Head in the country of the Corcu Roide, to which he gave an altar stone, and another at Cúl Corrae. He crossed the river Ethne[22] and came to the two Tethbi and consecrated Mel as bishop. He founded a church at Bile and consecrated Gósacht son of Miliuc moccu Bóin, whom he had brought up during his seven years as a slave. And he sent Camulacus of the Commienses to Mag Cumi and with his finger pointed out to him the place, that is the church of Raithen, from the hill of Granard. And he came to Mag Réin and ordained Bruscus as a priest and founded a church for him. Bruscus said something miraculous after his death to another holy man, who was in the monastery of the family of Cothirbe: " All is well with you for you have a son. I, however, hate my death because I am alone in a deserted church, a church abandoned and empty, and no priests offer Mass near me." For three nights he had this dream, then on the third he got up, took an iron shovel, and dug up the grave, then carried the bones of holy Bruscus with him to the monastery where they now are. After this Bruscus remained silent.

(17) Patrick sent Nieth Brain to the earthwork of Slecht. He was a barbarian close to Patrick who made miraculous true prophecies by the power of God. Then Patrick came to a place on the Shannon where his chariot driver Boidmal had died. He is buried there in a place that had been given to Patrick and is called the Wood of

22. *Ethne*: River Inny, County Westmeath.

primus in regionibus nepotum Neill peractus. Incipit secundus in regionibus Connacht peractus.

(18) Omnia quae scripsi a principio libri huius scitis quia in uestris regionibus gesta sunt nissi de eis pauca quae inueni in utilitatem laboris mei a senioribus multis ac ab illo Ultano episcopo Conchuburnensi, qui nutriuit me, retulit sermo. Cor autem meum cogitat in me de Patricii dilectione, quia uideo dissertores et archiclocos et milites Hiberniae quod odio habent paruchiam Patricii, quia substraxerunt ab eo quod ipsius erat timentque quoniam, si quaereret heres Patricii paruchiam illius, potest pene totam insolam sibi reddere in paruchiam, quia Deus dedit illi i. totam insolam cum hominibus per anguelium Domini ii. et legem Domini docuit illis iii. et babtismo Dei babtitzauit illos iiii. et crucem Christi indicauit u. et resurrectionem eius nuntiauit; sed familiam eius non dilegunt, quia i. non licet iurare contra eum ii. et super eum iii. et de eo iiii. et non lignum licet contra eum mitti, quia ipsius sunt omnes primitiuae aeclessiae Hiberniae, sed supraiuratur a se omne quod iuratur. Omnia autem quae scripsi ab initio libri huius semplicia sunt; omne autem quod restat strictius erit.

(19) Venit ergo Patricius sanctus per alueum fluminis Sinnae per Vadum Duorum Auium in campum Ai. Audientes autem magi Loiguiri filii Neill omnia quae facta fuerant Caluus et Capitolauium, duo fratres qui nutrierant duas filias Loiguiri Ethne alba <et> Fedelm rufa, timentes ne mores sancti uiri acciperent, indignati sunt ualde tenebrasque nocturnales ac densas inaurinas super totum campum Ai fecerunt. Nescimus cuius potestatis hoc fuit, sed scimus quod nox longua trium dierum tot et noctium erat. Arripuitque sanctus ieiunium tribus diebus et tribus noctibus cumque centenis oraculis flectenisque assiduis Deum regem regum rogabat, et discessit omnis grauitudo magica tenebrarum

Boidmal to this day. This is end of the first book of deeds performed in the territory of the Uí Néill. Here begins the second book of deeds performed in Connaught.

(18) You know that all the things I have written since the beginning of this book took place in your own regions, except for a few things I discovered in my research from many elders and from the bishop Ultán Moccu Conchubair, whom I mentioned earlier as the one who was my spiritual father. However my heart is stirred with love for Patrick, because I see deserters and wicked thieves and warriors of Ireland who hate the sacred jurisdiction of Patrick. They have stolen from him what is his and are afraid, for if an heir of Patrick were to claim what is his, almost the whole island would have to be returned to his jurisdiction. This is because, first, God gave him the whole island with its people as his domain. Second, he taught them the law of the Lord. Third, he baptized them with the baptism of God. Fourth, he showed them the cross of Christ. Fifth, he preached to them Christ's resurrection. But they do not love his community because, first, it is not permitted to swear against Patrick. Second, they may not overswear him. Third, it is not permitted to draw lots against him against him, because all the primitive churches of Ireland are his. He indeed overswears all that is sworn. Up until this point in my book, I have dealt with general matters, but now I will be more specific.

(19) So holy Patrick crossed the river Shannon at the Ford of the Two Birds going towards Mag Aí. But when the news reached the druids of Loíguire son of Níall, Calvus and Capitolauium, who raised the two daughetrs of Loíguire, fair-haired Ethne and red-haired Fedelm, they feared that the women might accept the ways of the holy man. The druids grew very angry and brought the darkness of night and a dense fog over all of Mag Aí. We do not know by whose power this was done, but we know that the darkness lasted three days and three nights. The holy man then began a fast of three days and three nights, so that with a hundred prayers and constant prostrations before God, the king of kings, all the evil magic

a campo Ai, et dixit "Deo gratias." Et uenierunt per alueum fluminis Sinnae quae dicitur Bandea ad Tumulum Gradi, in quo loco ordinauit Ailbeum sanctum praepiterum, cui indicauit altare mirabile lapideum in monte nepotum Ailelo, quia inter nepotes Ailello erat, et babtitzauit Maneum sanctum, quem ordinauit episcopus Bronus filius Icni seruus Dei, socius Patricii.

(20) Venierunt ad campum Glais et in illo posuit celolam magnam, quae sic uocatur Cellula Magna, et in illa reliquit duo barbaros Conleng et Ercleng monachos sibi.

(21) Deinde uenit ad Assicum et Bitteum et ad magos qui fuerunt de genere Corcu Chonluain, Hono et Ith fratres. Alter suscepit Patricium at sanctos eius cum gaudio et immolauit sibi domum suam. Et exiit ad Imbliuch Hornon, et dixit illi Patricius: "Semen tuum erit benedictum et de tuo semine erunt sacerdotes Domini et princepes digni in mea elimoysina et tua hereditate," et possuit ibi Assicum et Betheum filium fratris Assici et Cipiam matrem Bethei episcopi.

(22) Asicus sanctus episcopus faber aereus erat Patricio et faciebat altaria <et> bibliothecas quadratas faciebat in patinos sancti nostri pro honore Patricii episcopi, et de illis tres patinos quadratos uidi, id est patinum in aeclessia Patricii in Ardd Machae et alterum in aeclessia Alo Find et tertium in aeclessia magna Saeoli super altare Felarti sancti episcopi. Asicus iste fecit profugam in aquilonem regionis ad Montem Lapidis et fuit septem annis in insola quae uocatur Rochuil retro Montem Lapidum; et quaerebant illum monachi sui et inuenierunt eum in conuallibus montanis iuxta laborem artificiorum, et abstraxerunt eum monachi eius et mortuus erat apud illos in disertis montibus, et sepilierunt eum hirRaith Chungai hi Sertib, et dedit rex illi et monachis suis post mortem foenum centum uaccarum cum uitulis suis et bouum uiginti, immolatio aeterna, quia dixit quod non reuerteretur in campum Ai, quia mendacium ab illo dixerunt, et sunt ossa eius

of darkness disappeared from Mag Aí. And he said: "Thanks be to God." And he passed through the bed of the river Shannon that is called Bandea to Dume Gráid, where Patrick ordained Ailbe as a holy priest. He pointed out to him a marvelous stone altar on the mountain of Uí Ailello, for he was one of the Uí Ailello, and he baptized holy Maneum, whom Bishop Bronus, son of Icne, a servant of God and companion of Patrick, ordained.

(20) They came to Mag Glais and there he founded a large church called Cell Mór. There he left two barbarians, his monks Conleng and Ercleng.

(21) Then he went to Assicus and Bitteus and to the druids who were of the tribe of Corcu Chonluain, the brothers Hono and Ith. One of them welcomed with joy Patrick and his holy men and offered him his own house. And Patrick went out to Imlech Honon and said to him: "Your seed will be blessed and from your descendants will come priests of the Lord and heads of churches worthy of my revenue and your inheritance." And there he appointed Assicus and Betheus the son of Assicus' brother and Cipia the mother of bishop Betheus.

(22) The holy bishop Assicus was a coppersmith for Patrick and made altar plates and shrines for the patens of our saint in honor of bishop Patrick. I have seen three of these square patens, one in the church of Patrick at Armagh, another in the church of Ail Find, and the third at the great church of Seól on the altar of holy bishop Felartus. This Assicus took refuge in the northern region of near Slíab Líacc and stayed there at a hermitage which is called Rochuil beyond Slíab Líacc. His monks searched for him and discovered him in the mountain valleys with his metalwork. His monks took him away by force and he died with them in the lonely mountains. They buried him in Ráith Cungi in Mag Sereth. The king gave to him and his monks after his death grazing for a hundred cows with their calves and for twenty oxen, a grant in perpetuity, for he said he would not return to Mag Aí where they had lied about him. His bones are in Mag Sereth in Ráith Cungi. He was a monk of Patrick,

in campo Sered hirRaith Chungi. Monachus Patricii, sed contenderunt eum familia Columbae Cille et familia Airdd Sratha.

(23) Patricius uero uenit de fonte Alo Find ad Dumecham nepotum Ailello et fundauit in illo loco aeclessiam quae sic uocatur Senella Cella Dumiche usque hunc diem, in quo reliquit uiros sanctos Macet et Cetgen et Rodanum praespiterum.

(24) Et uenit apud se filia felix in perigrinationem nomine Mathona soror Benigni successoris Patricii, quae tenuit pallium apud Patricium et Rodanum; monacha fuit illis et exiit per montem filiorum Ailello et plantauit aeclessiam liberam hi Tamnuch et honorata fuerat a Deo et hominibus et ipsa fecit amicitiam ad reliquias sancti Rodani et successores illius epulabantur ad inuicem.

(25) Post haec autem posuerunt episcopos iuxta sactam eclessiam hi Tamnuch, quos ordinauerunt episcopi Patricii, id est Bronus et Bietheus; non quaerebant aliquid a familia Dumiche nissi amicitiam tantummodo, sed quaerit familia Clono, qui per uim tenent locos Patricii multos post mortalitates nouissimas.

(26) Deinde autem uenit sanctus Patricius ad fontem qui dicitur Clebach in lateribus Crochan contra ortum solis ante ortum solis et sederunt iuxta fontem, et ecce duae filiae regis Loiguiri Ethne alba et Fedelm rufa ad fontem more mulierum ad lauandum mane uenierunt et senodum sanctum episcoporum cum Patricio iuxta fontem inuenierunt. Et quocumque essent aut quacumque forma aut quacumque plebe aut quacumque regione non cognouerunt, sed illos uiros side aut deorum terrenorum aut fantassiam estimauerunt, et dixerunt filiae illis: "Ubi uos sitis et unde uenistis?" et Dixit Patricius ad illas: "Melior erat uos Deo uero nostro confiteri quam de genere nostro interrogare." Dixit filia prima: "Quis est deus et ubi est deus et cuius est deus et ubi

but the community of Colum Cille[23] and the community of Ardd Sratha claimed him.

(23) Patrick went from the well of Ail Find to the Mound of the Uí Ailello and founded in that place a church which is called Senchell Dumiche still today. There he left the holy men Macet and Cetgen and the priest Rodanus.

(24) And there came to him a blessed young woman on a pilgrimage. She was named Mathona, a sister of Benignus the successor of Patrick, and took the veil from Patrick and Rodanus. She was a nun to them and went out across the mountain of the sons of Aillil and established a free church at Tamnach. She was honored by God and men, and she made a pact of friendship with the successors on the relics of holy Rodanus, and she and his successors dined with each other in turn.

(25) After these things, they placed bishops in the holy church at Tamnach, whom the bishops of Patrick, Bronus and Bitheus, consecrated. They did not seek anything from the community of Dumech but friendship, though the community of Cluain claims them, since they hold by force many of Patrick's churches since the recent plague.

(26) Then holy Patrick came to the well which is called Clébach on the eastern slopes of Cruachu before sunrise and his company sat by the well. And behold, the two daughters of King Loíguire, fair-haired Ethne and red-haired Fedelm, came to the well to wash in the morning. They found the holy gathering of bishops there along with Patrick. The daughters did not know where the men came from or what was their nature or what tribe they were from or what region, but thought they were men of the Otherworld or gods of the earth or phantoms. And the maidens said to them: " Where are you from? From where have you come?" And Patrick said to them: "It would be better for you to confess our one true God that to ask about our tribe." The first girl said: "Who is this god and where is he and who

23. *Colum Cille*: St. Colomba, founder of monasteries in Ireland and Scotland, most notably at Iona.

habitaculum eius? Si habet filios et filias, aurum et argentum deus uester? Si uiuus semper, si pulcher, si filium eius nutrierunt multi, si filiae eius carae et pulchrae sunt hominibus mundi? In caelo an in terra est, in aequore, in fluminibus, in montanis, in conuallibus? Dic nobis notitiam eius, quomodo uidebitur, quomodo delegitur, quomodo inuenitur, si in iuuentute, si in senectute inuenitur?" Respondens autem sanctus Patricius Spiritu Sancto plenus dixit: "Deus noster Deus omnium hominum, Deus caeli ac terrae, maris et fluminum, Deus solis ac lunae <et> omnium siderum, Deus montium sublimium ualliumque humilium; Deus super caelo et sub caelo, habet habitaculum erga caelum et terram et mare et omnia quae sunt in eis; inspirat omnia, uiuificat omnia, superat omnia, sufultat omnia; solis lumen inluminat, lumen noctis et notitias ualat, et fontes fecit in arida terra et insolas in mari siccas et stellas in ministerium maiorum luminum posuit. Filium habet coaeternum sibi, consimilem sibi; non iunior Filius Patri nec Pater Filio senior, et Spiritus Sanctus inflat in eis; non separantur Pater et Filius et Spiritus Sanctus. Ego uero uolo uos regi caelesti coniungere dum filiae regis terreni sitis credere. Et dixerunt filiae <ac> si ex uno ore unoque corde: "Quomodo credere possimus caelesti regi doce nos dilegentissime, ut uideamus illum facie ad faciem. Indica nobis, et quomodo dixeris nobis faciamus." Et dixit Patricius: "Si creditis per babtismum patris et matris iecere peccatum?" Responderunt: "Credimus." "Si poenitentiam creditis post peccatum." "Credimus." "Si creditis uitam post mortem? Si creditis resurrectionem in die iudicii?" "Credimus." "Si creditis unitatem aeclessiae?" "Credimus." Et babtitzatae sunt et candida ueste in capitibus earum. Et postulauerunt uidere faciem Christi, et dixit eis sanctus: "Nissi mortem gustaueritis, non potestis uidere faciem Christi, et nissi sacrificium accipietis." Et responderunt: "Da nobis sacrificium, ut possimus Filium, nostrum sponsum, uidere," et acciperunt eucharitziam Dei et dormierunt in morte, et posuerunt illas in lectulo uno uestimentis coopertas, et fecerunt ululatum et planctum magnam

does he belong to and where is his home? Does he have sons and daughters? Does your god have gold and silver? Is he always alive? Is he beautiful? Have many people fostered his son? Are his daughters dear and beautiful to the men of this world? Is he in the sky or on the earth? Is he in water, in rivers, in mountains, in valleys? Tell us about him. How can he be seen? How is he loved? How can he be found? Is he young or is he old?" But Patrick, full of the Holy Spirit, answered her and said: "Our God is the God of all people, the God of sky and earth, the God of sea and rivers, of sun and moon and all the stars. He is God of the high mountains and low valleys. God is above the sky and in it and under it. He lives in the sky and earth and sea and in everything that is in them. He breathes into everything, makes everything alive. He rules all things, supports all things. He kindles the light of the sun, he gives light to the night and to the stars. He has made wells on dry land and dry islands in the sea and stars in the service of the greater lights. He has a Son coeternal with him, similar to him. The Son is not younger than the Father nor the Father older than the Son, and the Holy Spirit breathes in them. The Father and Son and Holy Spirit are not separate. I would like to join you with this celestial king since you are daughters of an earthly king, if you are willing to believe." And the girls said with one voice and one heart: "Teach us most diligently how we might believe in this heavenly king, so that we may see him face to face. Tell us and we will do as you say." And Patrick said: "Do you believe that through baptism you cast away the sin of your father and mother?" They answered: "We believe." "Do you believe in life after death? Do you believe in the resurrection in the day of judgment?" "We believe." "Do you believe in the unity of the church?" "We believe." And they were baptized with a white garment over their heads. And they demanded to see the face of Christ, so the holy one said to them: "Unless you taste death, you cannot see the face of Christ, unless you receive the sacrament." They answered: "Give us this sacrament so that we can see the Son, our bridegroom." And they accepted the Eucharist of God and fell asleep in death. Their

amici earum. Venit magus Caplit, qui nutriunt alteram, et fleuit, et illi Patricius praedicauit et credidit et capilli capitis eius ablati sunt. Et frater illius uenit Mael et ipse dixit: "Frater meus credidit Patricio; ***ta, sed reuertam eum in gentilitatem," et ad Mathonum <et> ad Patricium uerba dura dixit. Et Patricius illi de fide praedicauit et conuertit illum in poenitentiam Dei et ablati sunt capilli capitis illius, id est norma magica in capite uidebatur, *airbacc* ut dicitur *giunnae*. De hoc est uerbum quod clarius est omnibus uerbis Scoticis, "Similis est Caluus contra Caplit," quia crediderunt in Deo. Et consumpti sunt dies ululationis filiarum regis et sepilierunt eas iuxta fontem Clebach et fecerunt fossam rotundam in similitudinem *fertae*, quia sic faciebant Scotici homines et gentiles, nobiscum autem *relic* uocatur, <id est> residuae puellarum. Et immolata est *ferta* *** Patricio cum sanctarum ossibus et heredibus eius post se in saecula, et aeclessiam terrenam fecit in eo loco.

(27) Deinde autem uenit Patricius <ad> campum Cairetho, id est Maig Cairetho, et castrametati sunt <in eo loco>, et fundauerunt aeclessiam in Ardd Licce, quae sic vocatur: Sendomnach, et posuit in illa Coimanum diaconum, sanctum sibi monachum, carum Christo et Patricio puerum, et tenuit Patricius Ardd Senlis et posuit filiam in eo sanctam Lalocam et tenuit locum in campo Nento. <Et exierunt cum> Cethiaco sancto episcopo in suam propriam regionem, quia de genere Ailello <eius> pater fuit; mater eius erat de genere Sai de regionibus Cenachtae a Domnach Sairigi iuxta Domum Liacc Cennani, id est lapidum. Moris erat Cethiaco episcopo s* **f***set in loco Curcu Sai in pasca magno; in pasca secundo fiebat in loco Comgellae sanctae super Vadum Duarum Furcarum, id est Dá Loarcc iuxta Cenondas *** quia Cethiachi <monachi> dicunt <monacham> esse Comgellam Cethiacho.

friends laid them in a single tomb and made a lament and great keening. The druid Caplit who had fostered one of the girls came and wept. Patrick preached to him and he believed and the hair of his head was shaved. And his brother Máel came and said: "My brother has believed Patrick, but not I. I will convert him back to heathenism. And he spoke harsh words to Mathonus and Patrick. But Patrick spoke and preached and converted him to the penance of God. The hair of his head was shaved, that is, the part cut in the druidic way on his head, which is called *airbacc giunnae*.[24] From this comes the most famous of Irish sayings: "Bald and Caplit, same thing," since both believed in God. And the days of mourning for the king's daughters ended and they buried them next to the well of Clébach. They made a round ditch there in the manner of a *ferta*,[25] as was the way of the pagan Irish. But among us it is called a relic, that is, the remains of the girls. And the *ferta* was given to Patrick and his heirs with the bones of the holy girls forever. And he built a church of earth in that place.

(27) Then Patrick came to the plain of Cairith, that is, Mag Caire-tho, and they made a camp in that place. They founded a church called Sendomnach there in Ard Licce, and in it he placed the deacon Coimanus, his holy monk, a pupil dear to Christ and Patrick. Patrick held Árd Senlis and placed there the holy maiden Laloca. He also held a place in Mag Nento. And they went out with the holy bishop Cethiacus to his own home country, for his father was of the family of Ailill. His mother was from the kindred of Sai from the region of Cíanacht, from Domnach Sairigi, near the stone house of Ciannán. It was the custom of Bishop Cethiacus to celebrate Mass in Corcu Saí on Easter Sunday. On the second day of Easter he would stay in the church of holy Comgella at the Ford of the Two Forks, that is, Dá Loarcc near Kells with Comgella, because the monks of Cethiachus say that Comgella was a nun to Cethiachus.

24. *Airbacc giunnae*: the druidic style of tonsure from ear to ear.

25. *Ferta*: a mound over a burial place, while *relic* is from Latin *relinqua* ("remains").

(28) <Relictus est> ab illis Iostus diaconus quidam sanctus pene puer pusillus in <regione> et tenuit Fidarti. et dedit illi Patricius libros babtismatis et babtitzauit nepotes <Maini>, et in senectutue sua bona babtizauit Ceranum filium artificis quando senex ac plenus dierum fuit. Interest autem inter mortem Patricii et Cerani natiuitatem, <ut> peritissimi numerorum aestimant, centum quadraginta annorum, et babtitzatus est Ceranus ex libro Patricii a diacono Iusto populi in conspectu.

(29) Franci uero Patricii exierunt a Patricio uiri fratres quindecim cum sorore una. Nomina quoque uirorum nolo dicere nissi duo principes Bernicius et Hernicius episcopi, et sororis nomen Nitria; et multi loci illis dati sunt, et ignoro nissi unum, in quo est Bassilica Sanctorum, quia indicauit illis Patricius sanctus similitudinem loci et digito indicauit de cacumine Garad, <quando> uenierunt ad illum ut elegeret illis de locis quos inuenierunt; et fundauit Cethiacus aeclessiam Brer Garad. Quaedam filia <erat> quae ueniret per flumen Succae, et aridi pedes eius ac ficones.

(30) Venit uero Patricius ad Selcam, in quo erant aulae filiorum Briuin, cum multitudine episcoporum sanctorum. Castrametati sunt in cacuminibus Selcae et posuerunt ibi stratem et sedem inter lapides, in quibus scripsit manus sua literas, quas hodie conspeximus oculis nostris; et cum illo fuerunt Bronus episcopus, Sachelus, Cassanus, Brocidius, Lommanus frater eius, Benignus heres Patricii et Benignus frater Cethiaci de genere Ailello, qui tenuit cellolam Benigni in *** Bronus praespiter, Rodanus, +anorto+ a Patricio <et> Cethiaco, Felartus episcopus de genere Ailello et soror <eius et altera> soror quae fuit <in insola> in Mari <Conmaicne, quae> sic uocatur: Croch Cuile; et plantauit aeclessiam super stagnum Selcae +inscae+, et babtitzauit filios Broin.

(31) Et perrexit ad tramitem Gregirgi et fundauit aeclessiam in Drummai, et fontem fodiuit <iuxta eam> et non habet flumen

(28) They left behind them in the region a certain deacon named Iustus, who was little more than a boy, and he held Fidarte. Patrick gave him books of baptism and he baptized the Uí Maini. In his good old age he baptized Cíarán[26] the wright's son when he was an old man in the fullness of his days. Between the death of Patrick and the birth of Cíarán there was, according to the experts in chronology, 140 years. Cíarán was baptized from Patrick's book by the deacon Iustus in the sight of the people.

(29) However, the Franks of Patrick left him, fifteen brothers and one sister. I do not wish to give the names of the men except the two most important men, the bishops Bernicius and Ernicius, and the name of their sister, Nitria. And many places were given to them, though I know only one, where there is now the Basilica of the Saints. For holy Patrick pointed out to them what each place was like and with his finger pointed out the summit of Gair, when they came to him asking him to choose for them places which they had found. And Cethiacus established the church at Brer Garad. There was a certain girl there who crossed the river Suck, but both her feet and shoes stayed dry.

(30) Patrick came to Selc, where the sons of Bríon had their halls, along with a crowd of holy bishops. They made camp on the heights of Selc and made their resting place among the stones, on which he wrote letters with his own hand which we can see with our own eyes even today. With him were Bishop Brón, Sachelus, Cassanus, Brocidius, Lommán, his brother Benignus the heir of Patrick, Benignus brother of Cethiacus of the race of Ailill who held the small cell of Benignus in *** Bronach the priest, Rodanus *** from Patrick and Cethiacus, Bishop Felart of the family of Ailill and his sister and another sister who was in the monastery in Marc Conmaicne which is called Croch Cúile. He built a church above Loch Selcae and baptized the sons of Brón.

(31) And he continued on the road to Gregirge and founded a church in Drummae, and dug a well. No stream flows into it or out

26. Ciarán founded the famous monastery of Clonmacnoise on the river Shannon.

in se et de se, <sed> plenus semper. Patini eius et calix sunt in Cella Adrochtae <filiae> Talain, et ipsa accipit pallium de manu Patricii; et perexit ad filios Heric, et fuit illo loco in quo fiunt mulieres iuxta Vadum Filiorum Heric, et furati sunt equos illius, et maledixit illis dicens: "Semen uestrum seruiet semini fratrum uestorum," quod sic conprobatur. Et reuertebatur in campum Airthic et aeclessiam Senes posuit in eo campo et benedixit locum iTaulich Lapidum.

(32) Et exiit ad Drummut Cerrigi et inuenit duo uiros conflingentes, filios unius uiri, ad inuicem post mortem patris eorum, qui faber aereus erat de genere Cerrigi Airnen. Noluerunt diuidere hereditatem, et possitum erat lignum contensionis, quod uocatur *caam* apud gentiles, quod defunctum est in terra more campi, et arripuerunt gladios ancipites extensis manibus percutere frater fratrem pedibus erectis. Cum uero ueniisset illis Patricius uidens de longue quasi modum iugeris, aperuitque os suum et dixit: "Tene, Domine pater, posco, manus fratrum, ne faciant malum inter se;" et non potuerunt porregere manum aut collegere, sed fuerunt erecti quasi imagines ligneas, et benedixit eos ac praecipit illis et ait: "Facite amicitiam, dum fratres sitis, et quod uobis dixero, facite: sedete." Sederunt sicut Patricius dixit et immolauerunt agrum et bona patris eorum Patricio Deoque caeli; fundauit aeclessiam ibi, et in illo loco est Coonu artifex, frater <Sachelli> episcopi Bassilicae.

(33) Perrexit per diserta Cerrigi <Airni> in campum australem id est Nairniu, et inuenit Iarnascum sanctum sub ulmo cum filio Locharnach, et scripsit illi elimenta; et fuit apud illum ebdoma siue eo amplius uiris nouem aut duodecim, et plantauit ibi aeclesiam et tenuit illum abbatem, et fuit quidem Spiritu Sancto plenus. Post haec uenit cum Patricio ab Irlochir ab australi <uir> Medbu nomine et legit in Ardd Machae et ordinatus est in eodem

32.402 *quod...campi* after *erectis* in A.

of it, but it is always full. Patens and a chalice of his are in the church of Adrocht daughter of Talan, who received her veil from the hand of Patrick. And he proceeded to the sons of Ercc and was in the place where there are women beside the Ford of the Sons of Ercc. They stole his horses and he cursed them saying: "Your seed will serve the seed of your brothers," which is fulfilled. And he returned to Mag Airthic and founded a church on that plain and blessed a place called the Hill of the Rocks.

(32) And he went out to Drummut Cérrigi and found two men fighting each other, sons of one man, after the death of their father, a coppersmith of the tribe of Cíarrige Airnen. They did not wish to divide the inheritance, and so the wood of contention had been set, which is called *caam* among the pagans (it is defined as the on the ground as a field). They had taken up their two-edged swords with their hands raised and their feet wide apart, brother against brother. When Patrick came to them and saw from a long distance (about one *iugerum*[27]), he opened his mouth and said: "Hold the hands of the brothers, Lord Father, I beg you, and don't let them hurt each other!" And they were not able to stretch out a hand or bring it back, but were frozen in place like wooden images. Patrick blessed them and instructed them saying: "Make peace, since you are brothers, and what I will say to you, do—Sit down." They sat down just as Patrick said and offered the land and goods of their father to Patrick and to the God of heaven. He founded a church there and in that place is the craftsman Cúanu, brother of Sachellus, bishop of Baislec.

(33) Patrick continued his journey through the wastelands of Cíarrige Airni to the southern plain, that is, Nairniu. He found holy Iarnascus under and elm tree with his son Locharnach and he wrote an alphabet for him. He spent a week or more there with nine or twelve men and founded a church and appointed him as abbot, a man full of the Holy Spirit. After this a man from the south, from Irlochir, came with Patrick and his name was Medbu. He studied

27. *Iugerum*: about 240 feet.

loco <et diaconus> fuit Patricio de genere Machi praespiter bonus et fundauit aeclessiam in Imgoe Mair Cerrigi liberam monachus in Ardd Machae.

(34) Et perrexit Patricius ad fontem quod dicitur Mucno et fecit cellam Senes, quae sic uocatur, et fuit Secundinus solus sub ulmo frondosso separatim, et est signum crucis in eo loco usque in hunc diem. Et uenit per diserta filiorum Endi in *** Aian, in quo erat Lommanus Turrescus. Post multa tempora uenit *** Senmeda filia Endi filii Briuin et accipit pallium de manu Patricii et dedit illi munilia sua et manuales et pediales et brachiola sua <quod> uocatur *aros* in Scotica.

(35) Et perrexit ad regionem Conmaicne hi Cuil <Tolith> et posuit in ea aeclessias quadratas, quarum scio unam magnam aeclessiam Ard Uiscon in *** cellolam mediam, in qua <reliquit> sorores Failarti episcopi de genere Ailello <et> aliam cellam Sescin *** .ii. barbarii *** nominibus suis. Et uenit in campum Caeri et castrametati sunt i Cuil Core et plantauit aeclessiam in illo loco et babtitzauit multos.

(36) Et exinde exiit ad campum Foimsen et inuenit in illo duo fratres, filios uiri nominati Conlaid, Luchte et Derclaid, qui mittebat seruum suum, ut occideret Patricium. Lucteus autem liberauit eum, cui dixit Patricius: "Erunt episcopi et praespiteri de genere tuo, genus autem fratris tui erit maledictum et difficient in breui," et reliquit in illo loco Conanum praespiterum.

(37) Et exiit ad fontem Stringille in diseris et fuit super ipso duobus dominicis et exiit ad campum Raithin et exiit ad *firu* Humail du Achud Fobuir, in quo fiunt episcopi; et uenit ad illum sancta filia, quae pallium tenuit apud Patricium, et ordinauit filium patris illius Senachus et dedit nomen illi .i. est Agnus Dei, et episcopum fecit illum. Et ipse postulauit tres postulationes a Patricio: ut non peccaret sub gradu, et non uocaretur nomen eius super locum, et <quod> deesset de illius aetate super aetatem filii sui ueniret Oingus nomine; cui scripsit Patricius abgitorium in die qua ordinatus est Senachus. Patricius ordinauit aeclessiam in illo loco apud

at Armagh and was ordained in the same place and was a deacon of Patrick. He was of the tribe of Mache, a good priest and monk of Armagh, and he founded a free church at Imgoe Már Cérrigi.

(34) And Patrick went on to the well that is called Mucno and founded a cell which is called Senes. And Secundinus was there alone under an elm tree with rich foliage. There is a cross there in that place to this day. And he came through the waste lands of the sons of Énde to *** Aian, where Lommanus Turrescus was. After a long time *** Senmeda daughter of Énde macc Brion came and received the veil from the hand of Patrick and gave to him her jewelry, that is, anklets and bracelets which are called *aros* in Irish.

(35) And he went on to the territory of Conmaicne, to Cúl Tolith and founded in it churches of four sides, of which I know one large church, Ard Uiscon, in *** the middle cell, in which he left the sisters of the bishop Failart of the tribe of Ailill, and another cell, Secen *** two barbarians *** their names. And he came to Mag Caeri and they camped in Cúl Core and he founded a church in that place and baptized many.

(36) And he went out to the Mag Foimsen and found in that place two brothers, sons of a man named Conlaid, Luchte and Derclaid; who sent his servant to kill Patrick. Lucteus however rescued him. And Patrick said to him: "There will be bishops and priests from your family, but your brother's family will be cursed and will soon be extinct." And he left in that place the priest Conán.

(37) And he went out to the well of Stringell in the waste lands and remained there for two Sundays. And he went out to Mag Raithin and to the men of Humal, to Ached Fobuir, in which place there are bishops. And a holy maiden came to him who took the veil from Patrick. And he ordained the son of her father, Senachus, and gave him a new name, that is, Lamb of God, and made him bishop. And he requested three things from Patrick: that he would not sin after consecration, that the place would not be named after him, and that whatever years his son Óengus was lacking should be made up from his own. Patrick wrote out an alphabet for him on the day

filiam Mathonam nomine et dixit illis: "Erunt episcopi boni hic et de semine illorum erunt benedicti in saecula in cathedra hac." Ipsa est Ached Fobuir et missam Patricii acceperunt.

(38) Et perrexit Patricius ad montem Egli, ut ieiunaret in illo quadraginta diebus et quadraginta noctibus, Moysaicam tenens disciplinam et Heliacam et Christianam. Et defunctus est auriga illius hi Muiriscc Aigli, hoc est campum inter mare et Aigleum, et sepiliuit illum aurigam Totum Caluum et congregauit lapides erga sepulcrum et dixit: "Sit sic in aeternum, et uissitabitur a me in nouissimis diebus." Et exit Patricius ad cacumina montis super Crochan Aigli et mansit ibi quadraginta diebus et quadraginta noctibus, et graues aues fuerunt erga illum et non poterat uidere faciem caeli et terrae et maris quia Hiberniae sanctis omnibus praeteritis praesentatis futuris Deus dixit: "Ascendite, o sancti, super montem qui inminet et altior omnibus montibus qui sunt ad occidentem solis ad benedicendos Hiberniae populos." ut uideret Patricius fructum sui laboris, quia corus sanctorum omnium Hibernensium ad eum uenit ad patrem eorum uissitandum; et plantauit aeclessiam in campo Humail.

(39) Et uenit in regiones Corcu Temne ad fontem Sini, in quo babtitzauit milia hominum multa <et> fundauit aeclessias .iii.. Et uenit ad fontem Findmaige qui dicitur Slan, quia indicatum illi quod honorabant magi fontem et immolauerunt dona ad illum in modum dii. Fons uero quadratus fuit et petra quadrata erat in ore fontis (et ueniebat aqua super petram .i. per glutinationes) quasi uestigium regale, et dixerunt increduli quod quidam profecta mortuus fecit bibliothicam sibi in aqua sub petra, ut dealbaret ossa sua semper, quia timuit ignis exustionem; quia adorabant fontem in modum dii. Et indicata est Patricio causa adorationis, et ipse zelum Dei habuit de Deo uiuo, et dixit: "Non uerum quod dicitis, quod rex aquarum fons erat" (quia dederunt illi nomen "aquarum rex"). Et congregati sunt magi et gentiles regionis illius

Senechus was ordained. Patrick consecrated a church in that place of the maiden named Mathona and said to them: " There will be good bishops here and from their seed blessed people will come forever in this see." This is Ached Fobuir. And they received the mass of Patrick.

(38) And they proceeded to Mons Aigli to fast there for forty days and forty nights, following the example of Moses, Elias, and Christ. And his charioteer died at Muiresc Aigli, that is, the plain between the sea and Mons Aigli. There Patrick buried his charioteer Totmáel, and gathered stones for his tomb and said: "Thus let him be forever, and he will be visited by me in the last days." And Patrick went out to the summit of the mountain, Cruachán Aigli, and remained there forty days and forty nights. And birds were troublesome to him and he was not able to see the face of the sky and land and sea. Because to all the holy men of Ireland—past, present, and future—God said: "Climb, O holy ones, to the top of the mountain which rises above and is higher that all the other mountains to the west of the sun to bring blessings to the people of Ireland." This was so that Patrick might see the fruit of his labors, because the choir of all the holy men of Ireland came to him to visit his father. And he founded a church in Mag Humail.

(39) And he came to the territory of Corcu Temne to the well of Sine where he baptized many thousands of people and founded three churches. And he came to the well of Findmag, which is called Slán, because he had been told that druids honored the well and made offerings there as if it were a god. The well was square in shape with a rectangular cover of stone at its mouth (the water came out through the stone, that is, through the cementing like a royal trail). The unbelievers say that a certain seer had made a casket in the water under the stone so that his bones might always be whitened, because he feared being consumed by fire. Because of this they worshipped the well as a god. And Patrick was told the reason for the worship. But he had the zeal of God from the living God and said: "What you say is not true, that the well was the king of the

et multitudo multa nimis ad fontem et Patricius ait illis: "Eleuate petram; uideamus quid subest, si ossa an non, quia dico uobis: sub ea ossa hominibus non sunt; sed puto aliquid de auro et argento per glutinationem petrarum minime de uestris reprobis immolationibus;" et non potuerunt petram eleuare. Et benedixit Patricius et serui eius petram, et dixit Patricius multitudini: "Procul recedite paulisper, ut uideatis uirtutem Dei mei, qui in caelis habitat"; et erectis manibus eleuauit petram ex ore fontis et ponebat illam e regione super ora fontis, et est semper. Et nihil inuenierunt in fonte nissi aquam tantum, et crediderunt Deo summo. Et sedit iuxta lapidem procul quem infixit uir quidam, cui benedixit Patricius, Caeta siue Cata nomine; et babtitzauit illum et dixit illi: "Erit semen tuum benedictum in saecula." Cellola Tog in regionibus Corcu Teimne Patricii fuit; Cainnechus episcopus monachus Patricii fundauit eam.

(40) Et uenit sanctus Patricius per campos in regionibus Maicc Hercae in Dichuil et Aurchuil. Et uenit Patricius in Duchuil ad sepulcrum magnum magnitudinis mirae ingentemque longitudine, quod inuenit familia illius et magno stupore mirabantur pedes traxisse centum uiginti, et dixerunt: "Non cridimus hoc negotium quod esset homo longitudinis huius." Et respondit Patricius et dixit: "Si uolueritis, uidebitis eum," et dixerunt: "Volumus," et percussit baculo suo lapidem iuxta caput eius et signauit sepulcrum signaculo crucis et dixit: "Aperi, Domine, sepulcrum," et aperuit. Et uir surrexit magnus sanus et dixit: "Bene sit tibi, o uir sancte, quod suscitasti me etiam una hora a doloribus multis," et ecce fleuit amarissime et dixit: "Ambulabo uobiscum?" Dixerunt: "Non possimus, ut nobiscum ambulaueris, quia non possunt homines uidere faciem tuam prae timore tuo. Sed crede Deo caeli

waters" (for they called the well "the king of the waters"). The druids and pagans of the region and a great crowd had gathered together near the well and Patrick said to them: "Lift up the stone. Let us see what is under it, whether there are bones or not. For I say to you that under it are not the bones of a man. I think that there is some gold or silver from your wicked sacrifices that leaks through the cementing of the stones." But they were not able to lift the stone. And Patrick and his servants blessed the stone and Patrick said to the crowd: "Stay a little bit away for a while so that you may see the power of my God who dwells in heaven." And with his hands stretched out he lifted the stone from the mouth of the well and put it on the other side of the mouth of the well, where it remains always. And they found nothing in the well except water and they believed in the high God. And there sat next to the stone Patrick had fixed in the ground a certain man whom Patrick blessed. His name was Caeta or Cata. And Patrick baptized him and said to him: "Your seed will be blessed forever." Cell Tog in the regions of Corcu Teimne belong to Patrick. Cainnechus, a monk of Patrick, was bishop there.

(40) And holy Patrick came through the plains in the territory of Macc Erce in Dichuil and Aurchuil.[28] And Patrick came in Dichuil to a large tomb of remarkable size and huge length, which his people had found. They were amazed that it stretched for 120 feet, and they said: "We not believe that there could have been a man of such length." And Patrick answered and said: "If you wish, you will see him." And they said: "We do wish." And he struck the side of the tomb with the head of his staff and made over the grave the sign of the cross and said: "Open, Lord, the tomb." And it opened. And an enormous man arose, sound in body, and said: "May it be well to you, holy man, for you have raised me even for an hour from my many pains." And behold he wept greatly and said: "May I walk with you?" They said: "We can't have you come with us because people are not able to see your face without being afraid. But believe in the

28. This incident takes place near Ballina, County Mayo, where there are many large Neolithic tombs.

et babtismum Domini accipe, et non reuerteris in locum in quo fiebas; et indica nobis cuius es." "Ego sum Macc Maicc Cais Maic Glais, qui fui subulcus Lugir *ríg* Hirotae. Iugulauit me *fian maicc* Maicc Con in regno Coipri Nioth Fer." (anno centesimo usque hodie). Et babtitzatus est et confessionem Dei fecit et resticuit et positus est iterum in sepulcro suo.

(41) Et uenit in Album Campum in regionibus nepotum Maini et inuenit in illo signaclum crucis Christi et duo sepulcra noua, et de curru suo sancus dixit: "Quis est qui seputus hic?" Et respondit uox de sepulcro: "Ecce, sum homo gentilis." Respondit sanctus: "Cur iuxta te crux sancta infixa est?" et iterum respondit: "Quia uir sepultus est iuxta latus meum, rogauit mater eius ut signum crucis poneretur iuxta sepulcrum filii sui. <Sed> uir fatuus et insensatus posuit iuxta me. Et exilit Patricius de curru suo et tenuit crucem et euellabat de gentili tumulo et posuit super faciem babtitzati, et ascendit super currum et orauit Deum taciter. Cum dixisset "libera nos a malo," dixit illi auriga illius: "Quid," auriga illius inquit, "cur appellasti gentilem non babtitzatum uirum? Quia ingemesco uirum sine babtismo. Melior erat apud Deum illum benedicere uice babtismatis et effundere aquam babtismi super sepulcrum mortui." Et non respondit illi; puto enim ideo eum reliquit, quia Deus eum saluare noluit. Redeamus ad historiam nostram.

(42) Per Muadan uero uenit, et ecce audierunt magi filiorum Amolngid quod sanctus uir uenisset super eos in suas regiones proprias. Congregata est multitudo nimia magorum ad primum magum Recradum nomine, qui uoluit sanctum occidere Patricium, et uenit ad illos cum nouem magis indutis uestibus albis cum hoste magico; et uiderunt illum procul Patricius et Endeus filius Amolngid et Conallus Endi filius, quando babtitzauit Patricius

41.538 *Redeamus...nostram* after *non babtitzatum uirum* in A.

God of heaven and accept the baptism of the Lord, then you will not return to the place where you were. And tell us who you are." "I am the son of the son of Cass son of Glas. I was the swineherd of Lugar king of Hirota. The warrior band of the sons of Macc Con killed me in the reign of Coirpre Nie Fer" (a hundred years ago today). And he was baptized and made his confession of God and fell silent and was laid again in his tomb.

(41) And he came to Findmag in the territory of the Uí Maini and discovered there a cross of Christ and two new tombs. And from his chariot the holy man said: "Who is it that is buried here?" And a voice answered from the tomb: "Behold, I am a pagan." And the holy man responded: "Why has a cross been placed next to you?" And again the voice answered: "Because of the man who buried next to me. His mother asked that a cross be placed next to the tomb of her son. But a stupid and foolish man placed it next to me." And Patrick jumped down from his chariot and grabbed the cross and pulled it from the tomb of the pagan and put it over the tomb of the baptized man. Then he climbed back into his chariot and prayed quietly to God. When he had gotten to "Deliver us from evil" his charioteer said to him: "What happened?" asked the charioteer. "Why did you talk to the pagan man who was not baptized? I am troubled about the man without baptism. I would have been better before God to bless him, as in baptism, and to pour the water of baptism above the tomb of the dead man." And Patrick said nothing to him. For I think he left him that way because God did not wish to save him. Let us return to our story.

(42) He went across the river Moy, and behold the druids of the sons of Amolngid heard that the holy man had come upon them into their own territory. A great crowd of druids gathered about their chief druid named Recrad, who wanted to kill holy Patrick. And Recrad came to Patrick's party with nine druids dressed in white clothes and with a large number of other druids, to Patrick and Énde son of Amolngid and Conall son of Énde, when Patrick

multitudinem nimiam, cumque uidisset Endeus, surrexit <et> arripuit arma, ut magos repelleret, quia ab illis erant magi trans riolum aquae nimium quasi *** milia passuum. Missit autem Patricius Conallum filium Endi in obuiam magis, ut cognouissent illum, ne alium occiderent, et stetit iuxta magum filius in signum. Et ecce uir sanctus surrexit Patricius et eleuauit manum sinistram Deo caeli et maledixit magum, et cecidit mortuus in medio magorum eius, et exustus est ante faciem omnium in uindictae signum. Et dispersus est uulgus in totum campum Domnon, cum uiderunt omnes homines hoc miraculum, et babtitzauit multos in illa die; et ordinauit Mucneum sanctum, fratrem Cethiachi, et dedit illi libros legis septem, quos reliquit post se Macc Erce filio Maic Dregin. Et fundauit aeclessiam super siluam Fochluth, in qua sunt ossa sancta Mucnoi episcopi, quia Deus dixit illi ut legem relinqeret et episcopos ordinaret ibi et praespiteros et diaconos in illa regione, et benedixit Amolngid filium Fergussum, fratrem Endi, quia in agro ipsius uirtutem fecit.

(43) Et ecce quidam uir uenit ad illos nomine Macc Dregin cum filiis septem gentilibus et postulauit babtismum Dei a Patricio, et benedixit illum cum filiis et elegit unum filium ex ipsis, cui nomen erat Macc Ercae, et scripsit elementa et benedixit eum benedictione praespiteri. Et dixit pater filii: "Tedibit me, si tecum exierit filius meus," et ait Patricius: "Non erit ita, sed illum Brono filio Icni commendabo et Olcano." Extendit manum et indicauit ei locum in quo sunt ossa eius procul et digito suo signauit locum et crucem posuit ibi; et ecce .ii. filiae uenierunt ad Patricium et acciperunt pallium de manu eius, et benedixit illis locum super siluam Fochlithi.

(44) Et ecce Patricius perrexit ad agrum quod dicitur Foirrgea filiorum Amolngid ad diuidendum inter filios Amolngid et fecit ibi aeclessiam terrenam de humo quadratum, quia non prope erat silua. Et portauerunt ad illum mulierem infirmam habentem in

had baptized a great multitude. When Énde saw him, he rose and took up arms to drive away the druids, because the druids were separated from them by a large stream about *** miles. Patrick, however, sent Conall son of Éndi into the sight of the druid, so that they might recognize the druid and not kill another. And the son stood next to the chief druid as a signal. And behold the holy man Patrick lifted up his left hand to the God of heaven and cursed the druid so that he fell down dead in the middle of his druids. And he was consumed by fire before the sight of all as a sign of judgment. And the crowd dispersed over the whole of Mag Domnon when they all saw this miracle, and he baptized many on that day. And he ordained holy Mucneus, brother of Cethiacus, and gave to him seven books of law, which he gave afterwards to Macc Erce son of Mac Dregin. And he founded a church at the wood of Fochloth where the holy bones of bishop Mucnoe are, for God told him to stop studying the law and ordain bishops and priests and deacons in that territory. And Patrick blessed Fergus the son of Amolngid, brother of Énde, because on his land he performed the miracle.

(43) And behold a certain man came to them by the name of Macc Dregin with seven pagan sons and asked for the baptism of God by Patrick. And Patrick blessed him with his sons and chose one them, named Macc Erce, and wrote and alphabet for him and blessed him with the blessing of a priest. And the father said to Patrick: "It will trouble me if my son goes with you." And Patrick said: "It will not be thus, but I will entrust him to Brón son of Icne and to Olcán." He stretched out his hand and showed a place in the distance, in which now his bones are, and pointed out with his finger the place and he erected a cross there. And behold two daughters came to Patrick and took the veil from his hand, and he blessed for them a place in the wood of Fochloth.

(44) And behold Patrick went forward to the land which is called Foirrgea of the sons of Amolngid to divide it between the sons of Amolngid. And he built there a square church made of earth, since there was no forest nearby. And they brought to him a sick woman

utero infantem, et babtitzauit filium in utero matris (aqua babtismi filii ipsa est aqua commonis mulieris), et sepilierunt eam in cacuminibus aeclessiae desuper, et est sedes ipsius sancti iuxta aeclessiam usque in praesentem diem; et aedificauit aeclessiam quandam apud familiam in sinu maris .i. est Ros filiorum Caitni.

(45) Et reuersus est ad flumen Muaide de Vertrige in Bertrigam et eleuauit ibi lapidem in signaculum crucis Christi et dixit: "Ecce hic inuenietur aqua in nouissimis diebus et habitabitur a me," et fundauit aeclessiam iuxta fossam Rigbairt; et uenit in Muiriscsam apud Bronum filium Icni et benedixit filium, qui est Macc Rime episcopus, et scripserunt elimenta illi et Muirethacho episcopo, qui fuit super flumen Bratho. Et uenierunt trans Litus Authuili in fines Irai Patricius et Broonus et cum illis filius Ercae filii Dregin ad campum .i. est Ros Dregnige, in quo loco est cassulus Brooni, et sedens ibi cecidit Patricii dens, et dedit dentem Brono suo in reliquias. Et dixit: "Ecce mare ieciet nos de hoc loco in nouissimis temporibus, et exibitis ad flumen Slicichae ad siluam."

(46) Et exiit trans montem filiorum Ailello et fundauit aeclessiam ibi .i. Tamnach et Echnenach et Cell Angle et Cell Senchuae. Et exiit ad regiones Callrigi Tre Maige et fecit aeclessiam iuxta Druim Leas, et babtitzauit multos, et erexit <se> ad campum Ailmaige et fundauit aeclessiam ibi .i. Domnach Ailmaige, quia Patricius illic mansit tribus diebus et tribus noctibus. Et perrexit ad campum Aine et posuit aeclessiam ibi, et uersus est Euoi et in campum Cetni. Et maledixit flumen quod dicitur Niger, quia postulauit et nihil illi piscium dabant sancto; Drobaiscum autem benedixit, in quo tententur magni pisces siue piscium genus effectum est. Flumen Drobaisco non habuit ante pisces sed postea piscatoribus fructum dat. Et maledixit aliis fluminibus .i. est flumini Oingae et Saele, quia dimersi sunt duo pueri de pueris Patricii in Saeli, quapropter hoc factum in commemorationem uirtutis.

(47) Etiam intrauit in campum Sereth trans amnem inter Es Ruaid et mare, et fundauit aeclessiam hirRaith Argi et castrametatus

having a child in her womb and he baptized the son in the womb of the mother (the baptismal water was the water of the womb). And they buried her above the church on a hill. And the seat of the holy man is next to the church even today. And he built a church for the family in the bay of the sea, that is, Ros macc Caitni.

(45) And he returned to the river Moy from Bartragh and raised up there a stone cross and said: "Behold here will be found water in the last days and it will be inhabited by me." And he established a church beside the moat of Rigbart and came to the Muiresc to Brón the son of Icne and blessed his son, that is, the bishop Macc Ríme. And they wrote an alphabet for him and for the bishop Muirethach, who was at the river Braith. And they came to Trácht Authuili into the borders of Ira, Patrick and Brón, and with them the Macc Erce Maicc Dregin, to the plain, that is, Ros Dregnige, where the chasuble of Brón is. And while sitting there, a tooth of Patrick fell out. Patrick gave it to his own Brón as a relic. And he said: "Behold the sea will drive us from this place in the last days and you will go to the river Sligo to the forest."

(46) And he went out across the mountains of the Uí Ailello and founded a church there, that is, Tamnach, and Echenach and Cell Angle and Cell Senchuae. And he went out to the regions of Callrige of the Three Plains and built a church by Druim Léas. He baptized many and went to Ailmag and founded a church there, that is, Domnach Ailmaige, because Patrick remained there three days and three nights. And he proceeded to Mag Aine and founded a church there, then he turned to Euoe and to Mag Cetni. And he cursed the river called Dub, because the people gave him no fish when he asked. But he blessed the river Drowes, in which there are many large fish. However the fish were increased, the river Drowes had no fish before, but now yields a harvest to fishermen. And he cursed other rivers, that is, the rivers Oengae and Séle, because two boys who belonged to Patrick drowned in the Séle. It was done to preserve the memory of his miraculous power.

(47) And he came to Mag Sereth and crossed the river between Es Ruaid and the sea. He founded a church at Ráith Argi and camped

est in campo Sereth. Et inuenit quendam uirum bonum de genere Lathron et babtitzauit eum et filium tenerum cum eo, qui dicebatur Hinu uel Ineus, quia posuit illum pater in fana super collum eius, quia natus est in uia cum patre de monte ueniens; babtitzauit Patricius filium et scripsit illi abgitorium et benedixit eum benedictione episcopi; qui postea retenuit Assicum sanctum cum monachis suis in Ard Roissen, id est hirRaith Congi in campo Sereth in tempore regum Fergusso et Fothuid. Et fundauit aeclessiam in campo Latrain et aeclessiam magnum Sirdrommo, quam tenuit familia Daminse in Doburbur. Et perrexit *for* Bernas filiorum Conill in campo Itho et fundauit ibi aeclessiam magnam. Et exiit ad campum Tochuir et fecit aeclessia ibi, et in quo loco quidam episcopus uenit de genere Corcu Theimne ad eum de cellola Toch in regione Temenrigi i Cernu contra solis occassum, episcopus cum sorore una, monachi Patricii, et est locus eorum cum familia Clono et ingemescunt uiri loci illius.

(48) Peruenit Patricius per Sinonam tribus uicibus et septem annos conpleuit in occidentali plaga, et de campo Tochuir uenit in Dulo Ocheni et fecit septem aeclessias ibi. Et uenit in Ardd Sratho et Macc Ercae episcopum ordinauit, et exiit in Ardd Eolorgg et Ailgi et Lee Benndrigi; et perrexit trans flumen Bandae et benedixit locum in quo est Cellola Cuile Raithin in Eilniu, in quo fuit episcopus; et fecit alias cellas multas in Eilniu, et per Buas fluium foramen pertulit et in Duin Sebuirgi sedit supra petram, quae petra Patricii usque nunc, et ordinauit ibi Olcanum sanctum episcopum, quem nutriuit Patricius et dedit illi partem de reliquiis Petri et Pauli et aliorum, et uelum quod custodiuit reliquias; et reuersus est in campum Elni et fecit multas aeclessias quas Coindiri habent.

(49) Ascendit autem ad montem Miss Boonrigi, quia nutriuit ibi filium Milcon maccu Buain, Gosacht nomine, et filias duas eiusdem uiri, quando erat in seruitute septem annorum, et docuit illos in taciturnitate cum iuramento pro timore magi. Sed alia nocte uidit magus Miliuccc scintellas de ore Succeti fatui ignitas

at Mag Sereth. He found there a certain good man from the tribe of Lathru whom he baptized along with his young son named Hinu or Ineus. His father carried him in a bundle around his neck, for he had been born on the way with his father coming from the mountain. Patrick baptized the boy, wrote him an alphabet, and blessed him with a bishop's blessing. Later Hinu gave hospitality to holy Assicus and his monks at Ard Roissen, that is, in Ráith Congi in Mag Sereth in the time of the kings Fergus and Fothad. And Patrick founded a church at Mag Latrain and the great church of Sirdruimm, which is held by the community of Daminis an the river Doburbar. And he proceeded over the pass of the sons of Conall to Mag Itho and founded a great church there. He went to Mag Tóchui and built a church there. In that place a certain bishop came to him from Cell Toch in the land of Temenrige in Cerae in the west, a bishop with one sister, a monk and nun of Patrick. The community of Clúain now with difficulty holds that place.

(48) Patrick crossed the Shannon three times and spent seven years in the west. From Mag Tóchuir he came to Dul Ocheni where he built seven churches. He came to Ardd Sratho and consecrated Mac Ercae as bishop. He went out to Ardd Eolorgg and Ailge and Lee Benndrigi. He crossed the river Bann and blessed the place where the cell of Cúl Raithne now is in Eilne, where there was a bishop. He built many other cells in Eilne and passed across the river Buas. He sat on a rock at Dún Sobairche which is called "Patrick's Rock" even today. There he consecrated holy Olcanus as bishop, whom Patrick had fostered, and gave him part of the relics of Peter and Paul, and of others as well, along with a covering to preserve them. He then returned to the plain of Eilne and built many churches which are owned by the Coindiri.

(49) Patrick climbed Slíab Miss of the Bonrige, for it was there he fostered the son of Míliucc moccu Bóin, whose name was Gósacht, along with two daughters of the same man, when he lived as a slave there for seven years. He taught them under an oath of silence because he feared the druid. But one night Míliucc saw sparks flying

ascendentes in labia filii sui, et inflammatum est totum corpus filii sui, et de ore filii sui in ora sororum eius. "Cur," inquit, "o serue, malum fecisti filio meo in nocte quae praeteriit?" Respondit Succetus: "Domine mi, quid uidisti?" "Os filii mei replisti igne et filius meus labia filiarum repleuit et consumpti sunt omnes in cinerem et cinis eorum uiuificauit multos et quasi aues uolauerunt tecum et euomerunt uitalia sua frustra." Respondit Succetus: "Frustra uere euomerunt, id est domum magicam, quia dedi in ora eorum uerba Dei mei excelsi."

(50) Et exiit ad montem Scirte ad locum petrae, super quam uidit anguelum Domini stantem, et uestigium pedis illius usque nunc pene adest, cum ascendisset in caelum pedibus extensis de monte ad montem, dixitque: "Ecce nauis tua parata est, surge et ambula." Venit uero sanctus per Doim in regiones Tuirtri ad Collunt Patricii et babtitzauit filios Tuirtri. Relicta Machia uenit in Maugdornu et ordinauit Victoricum Machinensem episcopum et aeclessiam ibi magnam fundauit; et perrexit ad Loiguireum et Conallum filios Neill.

(51) Finito autem circulo exiit et fecit aeclessiam Iustano praespitero iuxta Bile Torten, quae est apud familiam Airdd Breccain, et fecit alteram hi Tortena orientali, in qua gens o Thig Cirpani, sed libera semper. Et perrexit ad fines Laginensium ad Druimm Hurchaille et posuit ibi Domum Martirum, quae sic uocatur, quae sita est super uiam magnam in ualle et est hic petra Patricii in uia. Exiit ad campum Lifi et posuit ibi aeclessiam et ordinauit Auxilium puerum Patricii exorcistam et Eserninum et Mactaleum in Cellola Cuilinn. Ordinauit Feccum Album iSleibti, et babtitzauit filios Dunlinge et erexit se per Belut Gabrain et fundauit aeclessiam hirRoigniu Martorthige et babtitzauit filios Nioth Fruich *itír* Mumae super Petram Coithrigi hiCaissiul.

from the lips of the fool Succetus[29] into the mouth of his son. The whole body of his son was set on fire and from his son's mouth the sparks went to his sisters. "Why, slave" he said, "did you do harm to my son last night?" Succetus answered: "Master, what did you see?" "The mouth of my son full of fire and with fire my son filled the lips of my daughters. They were all burned to ashes and then the ashes came back to life and flew like birds with you and vomited out their vital organs in a deception." Succetus answered: "It was truly deception that they vomited up, that is, their druidic heritage, for I gave into their mouths the words of my most high God."

(50) And Patrick went on to Slíab Scirte to the place on the rock where he had seen the angel of the Lord standing—the trace of his foot remains there even today—where he ascended to heaven, his feet stretching from one mountain to the other. And the angel had said: "Behold, your ship is ready. Rise up and walk." The holy man came through Toome to the country of Uí Tuirtri to Collunt and he baptized the Uí Tuirtri. He left Machia and came to Maugdornai. He consecrated Victorinus as bishop of Maigen and founded a great church there. Then he proceeded to the lands of Loíguire and Conall, sons of Níall.

(51) Having finished his circuit, he went out and built a church for the priest Iustanus near Bile Torten, which is held by the community of Ardbraccan. He built another in eastern Tortiu where the tribe of Tech Cirpáin lives, but it free forever. And he went out to the borders of the land of Leinster to Druimm Hurchaille and built there the House of Martyrs, as it is now called, on the great road in the valley. And there is Patrick's Rock on the road. He went out to Mag Lifi and built there a church and ordained Auxilius, a fosterling of Patrick, and Eserninus and Mac Táil in Cell Cuilinn. He ordained Fiacc the Fair in Slébte and baptized the sons of Dúnlang. Then he went through Belut Gabráin and founded a church in Roinge of the House of Martyrs and baptized the sons of Nie Froich in the land of Munster on Patrick's Rock at Cashel.

29. Tírechán uses Patrick's slave name and calls him a fool (*fatuus*) from the perspective of his old master.

DICTA PATRICII

(1) Timorem Dei habui ducem iteneris mei per Gallias atque Italiam, etiam in insolis quae sunt in mari Terreno.

(2) De saeculo requissistis ad paradissum. *Deo gratias.*[a]

(3) Aeclessia Scotorum, immo Romanorum, ut Christiani ita ut Romani sitis, ut decantetur uobiscum oportet omni hora uox illa laudabilis "Curie lession, Christe lession." Omnis aeclessia quae sequitur me cantet "Cyrie lession, Christe lession." Deo gratias.

2.3 Bieler (1979, 124) divides the second dictum into two separates sayings, but as O'Loughlin (2005, 184 fn. 3) points out, the author has simply reversed the order of this line taken from Patrick's *Letter* (17) in which *Deo gratias* occurs immediately before the rest of the saying, separated from it only by the words *creduli baptizati.*

a. Cf. Rom 6.17.

THE SAYINGS OF ST. PATRICK

(1) I had the fear of God as my guide on my journey through Gaul and Italy, even in the islands of the Tyrrhenian Sea.[1]

(2) You have gone from the world to paradise. "Thanks be to God."[2]

(3) The church of the Irish, rather, of the Romans, so that you may be Christians like the Romans, you should recite at every hour of prayer that praiseworthy chant: *Kyrie eleison, Christe eleison* ("Lord, have mercy. Christ, have mercy").[3] Let every church that follows after me sing: *Kyrie eleison, Christe eleison.* Thanks be to God.

1. This has been taken as a reference to the monastic island of Lérins off the coast of Provence, but this is rejected by Bieler (1953A, 95–96). Nonetheless, Tírechán (1) says that his teacher the Bishop Ultán told him that Patrick stayed on the island Aralanensis, often identified with Lérins, for thirty years before coming to Ireland.

2. A passage taken directly from Patrick's *Letter* (17), as is *Deo gratias* (*Letter* 17, *Confession* 19, 23, 42).

3. The Greek liturgical phrases *Kyrie eleison, Christe eleison* ("Lord have mercy, Christ have mercy") were used in the east by the mid-fourth century and introduced into the Eucharistic portion Roman Mass by Pope Gelasius I in the late fifth century, though they may have been present in the liturgy earlier (see O'Loughlin 2005, 184–185 fn. 4).

SINODUS EPISCOPORUM

Incipit sinodos episcoporum id est Patrici, Auxilii, Issernini. Gratias agimus Deo Patri et Filio et Spiritui Sancto. Presbiteris et diaconibus et omni clero Patricius Auxilius Isserninus episcopi salutem. Satius nobis neglegentes praemonere quae culpare que facta sunt Solamone dicente: *Melius est arguere quam irasci.*[a] Exempla difinitionis nostrae inferius conscripta sunt et sic inchoant:

(1) Si quis in quaestionem captiuis quesierit in plebe suo iure sine permisione meruit excommonicari.

(2) Lectores denique cognoscant unus quisque aecclesiam in qua psallat.

(3) Clericus uagus non sit in plebe.

(4) Si quis permissionem acciperit et collectum sit praetium non plus exigat quam quod necessitas poscit.

(5) Si quid supra manserit ponat super altare pontificis ut detur ali indigenti.

(6) Quicumque clericus ab hostiario usque ad sacerdotem sine tunica uisus fuerit atque turpitudinem uentris et nuditatem non tegat, et si non more Romano capilli eius tonsi sint, et uxor eius si non uelato captite ambulauerit, pariter a laicis contempnentur et ab ecclesia separentur.

(7) Quicumque clericus ussus neglegentiae causa ad collectas mane uel uespere non occurrerit alienus habeatur nisi forte iugo seruitutis sit detentus.

a. Sir 20.1 (*quam bonum est arguere quam irasci* in Vulgate).

THE FIRST SYNOD OF ST. PATRICK

Here begins the synod of the bishops, that is, of Patrick, Auxilius, Iserninus.[1] We give thanks to God the Father and the Son and the Holy Spirit. To priests and deacons and to all the clergy, the bishops Patrick, Auxilius, Iserninus, greetings. To us it is better to forewarn the careless than give blame afterwards. As Solomon says: "It is better to reason than be angry." Copies of our decisions have been recorded and are given below:

(1) If anyone in his own community of his own accord and without permission has attempted to ransom captives, he deserves excommunication.[2]

(2) Lectors should get to know the church in which each sings.

(3) There is to be no wandering cleric in the community.[3]

(4) If anyone has received permission and money has been collected, he should not receive more than is necessary.

(5) If any money is left over, let him put it on the bishop's altar so that it may be given to another needy person.

(6) Any cleric, from usher to priest, who has been seen without a tunic and does not cover the shame and nakedness of his body, and if he has not cut his hair in the Roman manner, and if his wife has gone about with her hair uncovered, then let them be held in contempt by the laity and separated from the church.

(7) Any cleric who when summoned does not come to morning or evening prayers shall be considered a stranger, unless he is detained by the yoke of slavery.

1. Auxilius and Iserninus traditionally joined Patrick as bishops early in his ministry.

2. Patrick writes to the tyrant Coroticus (*Letter* 14) of ransoming such captives.

3. The Latin *plebs* is taken as a Christian community, though De Paor (1993, 135) translates it as *tuath*, the secular tribal unit basic to early Irish society.

(8) Clericus si pro gentili homine fideiusor fuerit in quacumque quantitate et si contigerit, quod mirum non †potest†, per astutiam aliquam gentilis ille clerico fallat, rebus suis clericus ille soluat detitum. Nam si armis conpugnauerit cum illo, merito extra ecclesiam conputetur.

(9) Monachus et uirgo unus abhinc et alia aliunde in uno hospitio non conmaneant nec in uno curru a uilla in uillam discurreant nec adsidue inuicem confabulationem exerceant.

(10) Si quis incoeptum boni operis ostenderit in psallendo et nunc intermisit et comam habeat, ab ecclesia excludendus nisi statui priori se restituerit.

(11) Quicumque clericus ab aliquo excommonicatus fuerit et alius eum susciperit, ambo coaequali penitentia utantur.

(12) Quicumque Christianus excominicatus fuerit, nec eius elimosina recipiatur.

(13) Elimosinam a gentibus offerendam in ecclesiam recipi non licet.

(14) Christianus qui occiderit aut fornicationem fecerit aut more gentilium ad aruspicem iurauerit, per singula cremina annum penitentiae agat; impleto cum testibus ueniat anno penitentiae et postea resoluetur a sacerdote.

(15) Et qui furtum fecerit demedium peniteat, .xx. diebus cum pane, et si fieri potest rapta repraesentet; sic in ecclesiam renuetur.

(16) Christianus qui crediderit esse lamiam in saeculo, quae interpraetatur striga, anathemazandus quicumque super animam famam istam inposuerit, nec ante in ecclesiam recipiendus quam ut idem creminis quod fecit sua iterum uoce reuocat et sic poenitentiam cum omni diligentia agat.

8.25 *potest* is likely a corruption (Bieler, Faris).

(8) If a cleric has given a surety for a pagan in any amount and if, as is not surprising, that pagan defaults on the cleric using some trick, the cleric shall pay what is owed from his own resources. If the cleric resorts to armed combat, he shall justly be considered outside the church.

(9) A monk and a virgin, each from a different place, shall not stay together in one guest house, nor shall they travel from one town to another in the same vehicle, nor shall they carry on long conversations.

(10) If any man has made a good beginning singing psalms and then quits and lets his hair grow, he shall be excluded from the church until he returns to his former state.

(11) If any cleric has been excommunicated by someone and another receives him, both must do the same penance.

(12) If any Christian has been excommunicated, not even his alms are to be accepted.

(13) Alms given by pagans are not to be accepted by the church.

(14) A Christian who has committed murder or fornication or, in the manner of a pagan, has sworn before a druid,[4] shall spend a year in penance for each offense. When the year is complete, he shall come with a witness and be absolved by a priest.

(15) And he who has committed theft shall do penance for half a year, with twenty of these days on bread alone, and, if possible, return the stolen goods. Then he be restored to the church.

(16) A Christian who believes there is such a thing as a *lamia*[5] in this world—that is, a vampire—is to be anathemized for giving a living soul that reputation. He shall not be received back into the church until he has publically recanted the charge he has made and done penance with all diligence.

4. The druids were the native priests of pre-Christian Ireland.

5. In Greek and Roman folklore, a *lamia* was a female monster who fed on the flesh and blood of children (e.g. Hor., *Ars Poet.* 340). A *strix* or *striga* also occurs as a vampire (e.g. Ovid, *Fasti* 6.139).

(17) Uirgo quae uouerit Deo permanet kasta et postea nubserit carnalem sponsum excommonis sit donec conuertatur; si conuersa fuerit et dimiserit adulterium penitentiam agat et postea non in una domo nec in una uilla habitent.

(18) Si quis excommonis fuerit nec nocte pascharum in ecclesiam non introeat donec penitentiam recipiet.

(19) Mulier Christiana quae acciperit uirum honestis nuptis et postmodum discesserit a primo et iunxerit se adulterio, quae haec fecit excommonis sit.

(20) Christianus qui fraudat debitum cuiuslibet ritu gentilium excommunis sit donec soluat debitum.

(21) Christianus cui dereliquerit aliquis et prouocat eum in iudicium et non in ecclesiam ut ibi examinetur causa, qui sic fecerit alienus sit.

(22) Si quis tradiderit filiam suam uiro honestis nuptis et amauerit alium et consentit filiae suae et acceperit dotem, ambo ab aecclesia excludantur.

(23) Si quis presbiterorum aecclesiam aedificauerit, non offerat antequam adducat suum pontificem ut eam consecret, quia sic decet.

(24) Si quis aduena ingressus fuerit plebem non ante baptizat neque offerat nec consecret nec aecclesiam aedificet nec permissionem accipiat ab episcopo, nam qui a gentibus sperat permissionem alienus sit.

(25) Si que a religiosis hominibus donata fuerint diebus illis quibus pontifex in singulis habitauerit aecclesis pontificalia dona, sicut mos antiquis ordinare, ad episcopum pertinebunt siue ad ussum necessarium siue aegentibus distribuendum, prout ipse episcopus moderabit.

(26) Si quis uero clericus contruenerit et dona inuadere fuerit depraehensus, ut turpis lucri cupidus ab ecclesia sequestretur.

21.64 *imductum* in ms; *in iudicium* (Bieler).

(17) A virgin who has vowed to God to remain chaste and afterwards marries a spouse in the flesh is to be excommunicated until she changes her ways. If she repents and sends away the adulterer, she shall do penance and not live in the same household or settlement as him.

(18) If someone is excommunicated, he shall not enter the church even on Easter night until he accepts penance.

(19) A Christian woman who takes a man in proper marriage and then deserts her husband to join with another in adultery, she shall be excommunicated.

(20) A Christian who does not pay a debt, just like a pagan, shall be excommunicated until he pays what he owes.

(21) If a Christian is wronged by someone and calls that person into court to hear the case instead of before the church, that man shall be considered a stranger.

(22) If anyone gives his daughter in proper marriage to a man, then she loves another with her father agreeing and accepting a bride price from the other, both shall be put out from the church.

(23) If any priest builds a church, he may not offer mass there until his bishop consecrates it, as is right.

(24) If someone comes to a community he shall not baptize nor offer mass nor consecrate nor build a church until he has permission from the bishop. For whoever seeks permission from pagans shall be a stranger.

(25) If an offering is given by pious people on days when the bishop is in residence at a church, the offering shall be considered a pontifical gift, as is the ancient custom, and the bishop may keep it for himself or distribute to the needy it as he sees fit.

(26) But if a cleric is caught using the offering, he shall be cut off from the church for his shameful greed.

(27) Clericus aepiscopi in plebe quislibet nouus ingresor, baptizare et offerre illum non licet nec aliquid agere; qui si sic non faciat excommonis sit.

(28) Si quis clericorum excommonis <fuerit>, solus non in eadem domo cum fratribus orationem facit nec offere nec consecrare <ei> licet donec se faciat emendatum; qui si sic non fecerit, dupliciter uindicetur.

(29) Si quis fratrum accipere gratiam Dei uoluerit non ante baptizetur quam ut .xl.mum agat.

(30) Aepiscopus quislibet qui de sua in alteram progreditur parruchiam nec ordinare praesumat nisi permissionem acciperit ab eo qui in suo principatu est. Die dominica offerat tantum susceptione et obsequi hic contentus sit.

(31) Si quis conduxerit e duobus clericis quos discordare conuenit per discordiam aliquam prolatum uni e duobus hostem ad interficiendum, homicida congruum est nominari; qui clericus ab omnibus rectis habetur alienus.

(32) Si quis clericorum uoluerit iuuare captiuo, cum suo praetio illi subueniat. Nam si per furtum illum inuiolauerit, blasfemantur multi clerici per unum latronem. Qui sic fecerit excommonis sit.

(33) Clericus qui de Britanis ad nos uenit sine epistola, etsi habitet in plebe, non licitum ministrare.

(34) Diaconus nobis similiter qui inconsultu suo abbate sine litteris in aliam parruchiam adsentiat, nec cibum ministrare decet et a suo presbitero quem contempsit per penitentiam uindicetur. Et monachus inconsultu abbate uagulus decet uindicari.

Finiunt sinodi statuta.

(27) Whatever cleric comes into the community of a bishop shall not baptize or offer mass or perform any duties. If he does not obey this, he shall be excommunicated.

(28) If any cleric has been excommunicated, he shall pray alone and not in the same house as the brothers. He is not allowed to say mass or consecrate until he has made amends. If he does not do so, he shall be doubly punished.

(29) If one of the brothers wishes to receive the grace of God, he shall not be baptized until he has fasted forty days.

(30) Any bishop who goes from his own jurisdiction to another's shall not presume to ordain unless he has received permission from him who holds jurisdiction in the place. On Sunday he shall offer mass only if invited and shall be content in obedience.

(31) If one of two clerics who are at odds over some matter hires an enemy of the other to kill him, he is to be called a murderer. Such a cleric is to be considered a stranger by all righteous people.

(32) If a cleric wishes to help a captive, he shall do so with his own money. For if he steals that captive away, many clerics will be blamed because of one thief. Whoever does this shall be excommunicated.

(33) Any cleric who comes from Britain without a letter, even if he lives in the community, is not allowed to serve.

(34) Similarly, if a deacon comes to a different community without a letter and without permission from his abbot, he should not be given food and he shall be punished by the priest whom he has disobeyed. Also a monk who wanders without the permission of his abbot shall be punished.

The end of the statutes of the synod.

YMNUM SANCTI SECUNDINI

Ymnum Sancti Patricii

(1) Audite omnes amantes Deum sancta merita
uiri in Christo beati Patrici episcopi
quomodo bonum ob actum similatur angelis
perfectamque propter uitam aequatur apostolis.

(2) Beata Christi custodit mandata in omnibus
cuius opera refulgent clara inter homines
sanctumque cuius sequuntur exemplum mirificum
unde et in caelis Patrem magnificant Dominum.

(3) Constans in Dei timore et fide inmobilis
super quem aedificatur ut Petrus aecclesia[a]
cuiusque apostolatum a Deo sortitus est
in cuius porte aduersum inferni non praeualent.

(4) Dominus illum elegit ut doceret barbaras
nationes et piscaret per doctrinae retia
et de saeculo credentes traheret ad gratiam
Dominum qui sequerentur sedem ad ethereum.

(5) Electa Christi talenta uendit euangelica
quae Hibernas inter gentes cum usuris exigit.[b]
nauigi huius laboris tum opere praetium
cum Christo regni caelestis possesurus gaudium.

(6) Fidelis Dei minister insignisque nuntius
apostolicum exemplum formamque praebet bonis
qui tam uerbis quam et factis plebi praedicat Dei
ut quem dictis non conuertit actu prouocet bono.

a. Mt 16.18 b. Mt 25.14–30

THE HYMN OF ST. SECUNDINUS

The Hymn of Saint Patrick

(1) Hear everyone who loves God of the holy merits
of a man blessed in Christ, the bishop Patrick,
how because of his good ways he is like the angels
and because of his perfect life, he is equal to the apostles.

(2) The blessed teachings of Christ he keeps in every way,
his works shine brightly among all people,
they follow his holy and wondrous example,
and thus praise the Father and Lord in the heavens.

(3) Constant in his fear of God and unshakable in faith,
on him the church is built as on Peter,
he has received his apostleship from God,
the gates of hell will not prevail against him.

(4) The Lord has chosen him to teach the barbarians
and to fish with the net of doctrine,
and from the world to draw believers to grace,
those who would follow the Lord to his heavenly seat.

(5) He sells the chosen talents of Christ's gospel
which he collects with interest among the Irish pagans,
as a reward of his labor on his journey,
he will have the joy of Christ's reign in the heavens.

(6) A faithful minister of God and his distinguished messenger,
he brings to good people the model and example of the apostles,
for he preaches the word of God in speech and in deeds,
so that the one not moved by speech is converted by actions.

(7) Gloriam habet cum Christo honorem in saeculo
qui ab omnibus ut Dei ueneratur angelus
quem Deus misit ut Paulum ad gentes apostolum
ut hominibus ducatum praeberet regno Dei.

(8) Humilis Dei ob metum spiritu et corpore
super quem bonum ob actum requiescit Dominus
cuiusque iusta in carne Christi portat stigmata[c]
in cuius sola sustentans gloriatur in cruce.

(9) Impiger credentes pascit dapibus caelestibus
ne qui uidentur cum Christo in uia deficiant
quibus erogat ut panes uerba euangelica
in cuius multiplicantur ut manna in manibus.[d]

(10) Kastam qui custodit carnem ob amorem Domini
quam carnem templum parauit sanctoque Spiritui
a quo constanter cum mundis possedetur actibus
quam et hostiam placentem uiuam offert Domino.[e]

(11) Lumenque mundi accensum ingens euangelicum[f]
in candellabro leuatum toto fulgens saeculo
ciuitas regis munita supra montem possita
copia in qua est multa quam Dominus possedet.

(12) Maximus namque in regno caelorum uocabitur
qui quod uerbis docet sacris factis adimplet bonis
bono praecedit exemplo formamque fidelium
mundoque in corde habet ad Deum fiduciam.

(13) Nomen Domini audenter adnuntiat gentibus
quibus lauacri salutis aeternam dat gratiam
pro quorum orat delictis ad Deum cotidie
pro quibus ut Deo dignas immolatque hostias.

c. Gal 6.17 d. Ex 16.31 e. Rom 12.1 f. Mt 5.14–16

(7) Glory he has with Christ, honor in the world,
who is venerated by all as an angel of God,
whom God sent, as he did Paul, an apostle to the gentiles,
so that he might guide people to the kingdom of God.

(8) Humble he is in spirit and body because of the fear of God,
the Lord delights in him because of his good deeds,
on his body he bears the holy marks of Christ,
the glory of the cross alone sustains him.

(9) Diligently he feeds believers on the heavenly banquet,
lest those who are seen with Christ should faint on the journey,
he gives to them like bread the words of the gospel,
in whose hands they are multiplied like manna.

(10) He keeps his body pure because of his love for God,
a body he has prepared as a temple for the Holy Spirit,
by whom constantly he is possessed by pure actions,
which he offers as a living sacrifice to the Lord.

(11) He is the light of the world, the shining one of the gospel,
raised up on a candlestick, shining out on the whole world,
he is the secure city of the king on a mountaintop,
which possesses great abundance of the Lord.

(12) He will be called the greatest in the kingdom of God
who fulfils with good deeds the holy words he preaches,
who puts forth by his good example the essence of the faithful,
and in a pure heart has confidence in God.

(13) He boldly proclaims the word of God to the pagans,
and gives them eternal grace in the baptism of salvation,
he prays to God daily for their sins,
for them he offers sacrifices worthy to God.

(14) Omnem pro diuina lege mundi spernit gloriam
qui cuncta ad cuius mensam aestimat quiscilia
nec ingruenti mouetur mundi huius fulmine
sed in aduersis laetatur cum pro Christo patitur.

(15) Pastor bonus et fidelis gregis euangelici
quem Deus Dei elegit custodire populum
suamque pascere plebem diuinis dogmatibus
pro qua a Christi exemplo suam tradit animam.

(16) Quem pro meretis saluator prouexit pontificem
ut in caelesti moneret clericos militiae
caelestem quibus annonam erogat cum uestibus
quod in diuinis inpletur sacrisque affatibus.

(17) Regis nuntius inuitans credentes ad nuptias[g]
qui ornatur uestimento nuptiali indutus
qui caeleste haurit uinum in uassis caelestibus
propinnansque Dei plebem spiritale poculum.

(18) Sacrem inuenit thesaurem sacro in uolumine
saluatorisque in carne deitatem peruidet
quem thesaurum emit sanctis perfectisque meritis
Israel uocatur huius anima uidens Deum.

(19) Testis Domini fidelis in lege catholica
cuius uerba sunt diuinis condida oraculis
ne humanae putent carnes aessaeque a uermibus
sed caelesti salleantur sapore ad uictimam.

(20) Verus cultor et insignis agri euangelici
cuius semina uidentur Christi euangelia
quae diuino serit ore in aures prudentium
quorumque corda ac mentes sancto arat Spiritu.

g. Mt 22.3

(14) For the glory of God he spurns the riches of this world,
all such things he ranks as nothing compared to God's table,
he is not moved by the violent clashes of this world,
but suffering for Christ, he glories in adversity.

(15) He is a good and faithful shepherd of gospel's flock,
whom God has chosen to guard his people,
and to feed his people with divine teaching,
for whom he gives his life, according to the example of Christ.

(16) The savior has raised him to great office because of his merits,
so that he train clerics as a heavenly army,
giving them heavenly nourishment along with their vestments,
which are covered by divine and sacred words.

(17) He is the messenger of the king, inviting believers to the wedding,
he is richly clothed in the wedding garment,
he drinks celestial wine from heavenly vessels,
and gives the people of God a spiritual cup.

(18) He finds a holy treasure in the sacred book,
sees the divinity in the flesh of the savior,
this treasure he has bought with holy and righteous works,
"Israel" his soul is called, for he sees Gods.[1]

(19) He is a faithful witness of the Lord to the universal law,
his words are sprinkled with divine oracles,
lest human flesh decay, eaten by worms,
but be salted with celestial flavor for sacrifice.

(20) A true and famous farmer of the gospel's fields,
his seeds are seen to be the gospel of Christ,
which he sows from his divine mouth into the ears of the wise,
whose hearts and minds he plows with the Holy Spirit.

1. Patrick is given this name based on the etymology of *Israel* as "seeing God" in Jerome (*On Hebrew Names* 13.21) and other early Christian writers.

(21) Christus illum sibi elegit in terris uicarium
qui de gemino captiuos liberat seruitio
plerosque de seruitute quos redemit hominum
innumeros de zaboli absoluit dominio.

(22) Ymnos cum apocalipsi salmosque cantat Dei
quosque ad aedificandum Dei tractat populum
quam legem in trinitate sacri credit nominis
tribusque personis unam docetque substantiam.

(23) Zona Domini praecinctus diebus ac noctibus
sine intermissione Deum orat Dominum
cuius ingentis laboris percepturus praemium
cum apostolis regnabit sanctus super Israel.

(21) Christ chose him to be his vicar on earth,
who frees captives from a double bondage,
he has redeemed many from human servitude,
and liberated countless people from the rule of the devil.

(22) He sings hymns, and the Apocalypse,[2] and the psalms of God,
he explains them for the edification of the people of God,
he believes in the law of the sacred Trinity,
and teaches that in three persons there is a single substance.

(23) He has girded himself with the belt of the Lord day and night,
without ceasing he prays to the Lord God,
he will receive the reward of his great labors,
when he rules over Israel with the apostles.

2. Also known as *Revelation*, the final book in the New Testament.

LORICA SANCTI PATRICII

Patraicc dorone in nimmunsa. I naimeir Loegaire meic Néil dorigned. Fád a dénma immorro dia diden cona manchaib ar náimdib in báis robátar i netarnid arna cleirchib. Ocus is luirech hirse inso fri himdegail cuirp 7 anma ar demnaib 7 dúinib 7 dualchib. Cech duine nosgéba cech dia co ninnithem léir i nDia, ní thairisfet demna fria gnúis, bid ditin dó ar cech neim 7 format, bid coemna dó fri dianbas, bid lúrech dia anmain iarna étsecht. Patraicc rochan so intan dorata na etarnaidi ara chinn ó Loegaire, na digsed do silad chreitme co Temraig; conid annsin atchessa fiad lucht na netarnade comtis aige alta 7 iarróe ina ndiaid .i. Benen; 7 fáeth fiada a hainm.

(1) Atomriug indiu
niurt trén togairm trindóit
cretim treodatad
fóisitin oendatad
in dúleman dail.

(2) Atomriug indiu
niurt gene Crist cona bathius
niurt a chrochtho cona adnacul
niurt a essérgi cona fresgabáil
niurt a thóiniuda fri brithemnas mbrátho.

ST. PATRICK'S BREASTPLATE

Patrick made this hymn. It was made in the days of Loegaire son of Niall.[1] The cause of its composition was to protect him and his monks against the deadly perils that awaited them. This is a breastplate of faith for protection of body and soul against devils and men and evils. When anyone shall repeat it daily with diligent intentions towards God, devils will not dare to face him. It shall protect him against all poisons and envy, it shall be a defense for him against sudden death, and it shall be a breastplate to his soul after death. Patrick sang this hymn when Loegaire laid an ambush for him[2] to keep him from going to Tara[3] and sowing the faith. It seemed to those lying in wait that they were wild deer with a fawn, i.e. Benén, following behind them. The name of the prayer is "The Deer Cry."

(1) I rise today
with a mighty strength, an invocation of the Trinity,
believing in the threeness,
confessing the oneness,
of the creator of creation.

(2) I rise today
through the strength of Christ with his baptism,
through the strength of his crucifixion with his burial,
through the strength of his resurrection with his ascension,
through the strength of his descent for the final judgment.

1. Loegaire, son of Niall of the Nine Hostages, was according to Muirchú (1.10) and Tírechán (1), was high king of Ireland when Patrick arrived to convert the island.

2. V. Muirchú 1.18.

3. Tara, in County Meath, was the traditional seat of the high kings of Ireland.

(3) Atomriug indiu
niurt gráid Hiruphin
i nerlattaid aingel
i frestul na narchaingel
hi frescisin esséirgi ar chenn fochraicce
i nernaigthib huasalathrach
i tairchetlaib fáthe
hi praiceptaib apstal
i nhiresaib fóismedach
i nenccai nóebingen
i ngnímaib fer fírien

(4) Atomriug indiu
niurt nime
soilse gréne
etrochtae ésci
áne thened
déne lóchet
lúathe gáithe
fudomnae maro
tairismige thalman
cobsaide ailech.

(5) Atomriug indiu
niurt Dé dom lúamairecht
cumachtae nDé dom chumgabail
ciall Dé domm imthús
roscc nDé dom reimcise
cluas Dé dom étsecht
briathur Dé dom erlabrai
lám Dé domm imdegail
intech Dé dom remthechtas
sciath Dé dom imditin
sochraite Dé domm anacul
ar intledaib demnae

(3) I rise today
through the strength of the love of the cherubim,
in the obedience of angels,
in the service of archangels,
in hope of the resurrection to gain reward,
in the prayers of the patriarchs,
in the predictions of the prophets,
in the preaching of the apostles,
in the faith of the confessors,
in the purity of holy virgins,
in the deeds of righteous men.

(4) I rise today
through the strength of the sky,
through the radiance of the sun,
through the light of the moon,
through the brilliance of fire,
through the speed of lightning,
through the swiftness of the wind,
through the depth of the sea,
through the steadiness of earth,
through the firmness of rock.

(5) I rise today,
with the strength of God to lead me,
with the wisdom of God to guide me,
with the eye of God to see before me,
with the ear of God to listen for me,
with the word of God to speak for me,
with the hand of God to guard me,
with the path of God to stretch before me,
with the shield of God to protect me,
with the army of God to stand before me,
against the traps of the devil,
against the temptations of sin,

ar aslagib dualche
ar irnechtaib aicnid
ar cech nduine mídúthrastar dam
i ceín 7 i nocus
i núathud 7 hi sochaidi.

(6) Tocuiriur etrum indiu inna huli nert so
fri cech nert namnas nétrocar fristái dom churp ocus domm anmain
fri tinchetla saibfáthe
fri dubrechtu gentliuchtae
fri sáibrechtu heretecdae
fri himchellacht nidlachtae
fri brichtu ban 7 gobann 7 druad
fri cech fiss arachuiliu corp 7 anmain duini.
Crist domm imdegail indiu
ar neim ar loscud
ar bádud ar guin
condomthair ilar fochraice
Crist lim, Crist reum, Crist im degaid,
Crist indium, Crist íssum, Crist úasum,
Crist dessum, Crist tuathum,
Crist illius, Crist isius, Crist inerus,
Crist i cridiu cech duini rodomscrútadar,
Crist i ngin cech óin rodomlabrathar,
Crist hi cech ruse nomdercaedar,
Crist hi cech cluais rodomchloathar.

(7) Atomriug indiu
niurt trén togairm tríndóit
cretim treodatad
fóisitin óendatad
in dúleman dail.

against the weakness of my nature,
against all who wish me ill,
whether I am far or near,
alone or in a crowd.

(6) I call today on all these power to protect me,
from the cruel forces that may attack my body and soul,
from the incantations of false prophets,
from the dark magic of pagans,
from the misleading ways of heretics,
from the snares of idolatry,
from the spells of women,[4] blacksmiths,[5] and druids,
from all that attacks the body and soul.
Christ protect me today,
from poison and fire,
from water and wounds,
so that I may gain my fullness of rewards.
Christ beside me, Christ before me, Christ behind me,
Christ within me, Christ beneath me, Christ above me,
Christ on my right, Christ on my left,
Christ in breadth, Christ in length, Christ in height,
Christ in the heart of everyone who thinks of me,
Christ in the mouth of everyone who speaks of me,
Christ in every eye that sees me,
Christ in every ear that hears me

(7) I rise today
with a mighty strength, an invocation of the Trinity,
believing in the threeness,
confessing the oneness,
of the creator of creation.

4. The Irish phrase *brichtu ban* ("the magic of women") is almost identical to the words (*bnas brictom*) from a first-century AD Gaulish cultic inscription from Larzac in southern France.

5. Blacksmiths were considered to have magical powers in Celtic and other northern European cultures.

INDEX SCRIPTURISTICUS

Index entries are keyed to the paragraph numbers in their respective works.

Old Testament

New Testament

GENERAL INDEX

Index entries are keyed to the paragraph numbers in their respective works.

General Index

General Index

General Index

INDEX OF MODERN AUTHORS